Scholastic World Cultures

JAPAN

by Ira Peck

SECOND EDITION

Consultant

H. PAUL VARLEY

Professor of Japanese Language and History
Columbia University

SCHOLASTIC INC.

Titles in This Series
CANADA
CHINA
GREAT BRITAIN
THE INDIAN SUBCONTINENT
JAPAN
LATIN AMERICA
MEXICO
THE MIDDLE EAST
SOUTHEAST ASIA
THE SOVIET UNION AND EASTERN EUROPE
TROPICAL AND SOUTHERN AFRICA
WESTERN EUROPE

ISBN 0-590-34635-0

Copyright © 1986,1981 by Scholastic Inc.
All rights reserved.
Published by Scholastic Inc.
Printed in the U.S.A.
12 11 10 9 8 7
1 2 3/9
23

Ira Peck is a professional writer. He has worked as a newspaper reporter and magazine editor. More recently he has written several books, including *The Life and Works of Martin Luther King* and *Patton*.

General Editor for World Cultures Program: Carolyn Jackson
Special Editor: Elise Bauman
Associate Editors: John Nickerson, LeRoy Hayman
Teaching Guide Editor: Frances Plotkin

Art Director and Designer: Irmgard Lochner
Photo Editor: Linda Sykes
Maps: Wilhelmina Reyinga

COVER: Flowerlike in their simple beauty, these traditional Japanese parasols are handcrafted on Kyushu Island.

JAPAN

Table of Contents

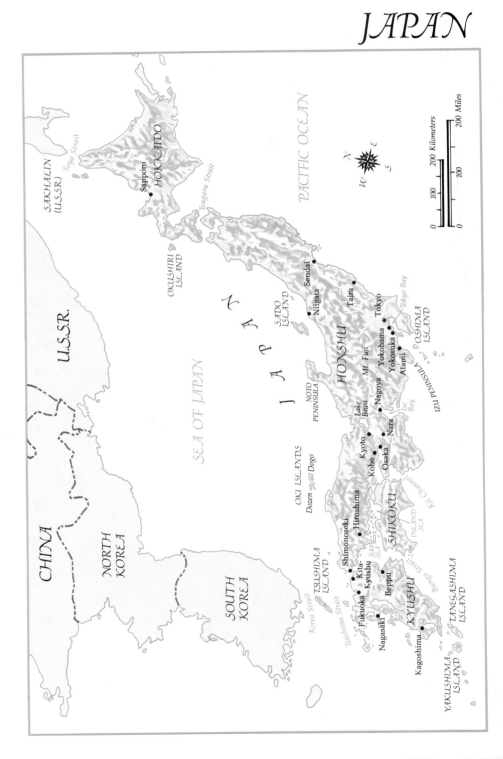

JAPAN

SAKHALIN
(U.S.S.R.)

Soya Strait

HOKKAIDO

Sapporo

PACIFIC OCEAN

200 Kilometers
200 Miles
100
100
0
0

OKUSHIRI
ISLAND

Tsugaru Strait

U.S.S.R.

SADO ISLAND

Sendai

Niigata

Taira

Tokyo

Tokyo Bay

J A P A N

HONSHU

Mt. Fuji
Yokohama
Yokosuka
Atami

OSHIMA ISLAND

SEA OF JAPAN

NOTO PENINSULA

Nagoya

IZU PENINSULA

Ise Bay

CHINA

NORTH KOREA

Lake Biwa

Kyoto
Kobe
Osaka

Nara

OKI ISLANDS
Dozen
Dogo

SHIKOKU

Kii Channel

SOUTH KOREA

Hiroshima

INLAND SEA

Bungo Strait

TANEGASHIMA ISLAND

Shimonoseki

Kita-
Kyushu

Beppu

TSUSHIMA ISLAND

Korea Strait

Fukuoka

KYUSHU

Tsushima Strait

Nagasaki

Kagoshima

YAKUSHIMA ISLAND

~§ *"The twenty-first century may not be 'the Japanese century,' as some non-Japanese have so grandiloquently proclaimed, but Japan may well be among the leaders — possibly even the preeminent leader — in finding solutions to the problems that mankind will face in the twenty-first century."*

EDWIN O. REISCHAUER,
FORMER UNITED STATES AMBASSADOR TO JAPAN

1
PEOPLE AND LAND

Chapter 1

A Growing Industrial Giant

"BULLET TRAINS" HURTLE between cities at 120 miles
an hour. Giant bridges and tunnels span the waters between the nation's main islands. High-speed freeways cut
through cities and mountains. Huge department stores
and shopping centers teem with well-dressed people.
Modern factories turn out a flood of high-quality, eco-
nomical products. These are sold all over the world.
Among them are motorcycles, cars and trucks, cameras,
and television sets.

A booming economy. This is Japan today — a modern industrial society that ranks behind only the United
States and the Soviet Union in the total production of
goods. Japan's economic growth since 1950 has astonished the rest of the world. In the 1960's, Japan's total
output increased at an astounding rate of 10 percent a
year, far more than any other nation's. Japan already
produces more than half of the world's merchant ships
and is third in production of steel, third in motor vehi-
cles, and second in electronic equipment. Japan's foreign
trade has also increased by leaps and bounds. Today Ja-

pan is either the largest, or second largest, trading partner of almost all of its neighbors in the Far East. If present trends continue, Japan's economy could rank first in the world by the end of the century.

Japan's people are enjoying a prosperity that not long ago was only a dream. Since the 1960's, the Japanese have been buying washing machines, refrigerators, stereos, TV sets, air conditioners, and cars in record quantities. They have taken up golf, skiing, and bowling, and are traveling all over the world as tourists.

Japan's prosperity has been matched by other achievements. The nation has a low crime rate and practically no drug problem. School dropouts are rare. About 90 percent of its young people graduate from senior high school, a proportion that may be the highest in the world.

Japan has also been enjoying a cultural and an artistic boom. Tokyo* alone supports five symphony orchestras. Japanese musicians, architects, moviemakers, and writers have won international acclaim.

The price of prosperity. Outwardly, at least, Japan impresses visitors as a healthy society. Its people appear to be cheerful, energetic, and determined. Does all this mean that the Japanese people have no problems? Are they "sitting pretty," enjoying the fruits of their prosperity? Life is never that simple. While the growth of industry has raised living standards, it has created some problems. Japan's cities have become terribly overcrowded. The air and waters are heavily polluted. The death toll from traffic accidents has risen sharply. Many Japanese are concerned about the decline of their old traditions. Among these traditions are family loyalties, ideas of duty and obligations, and respect for authority. People are

Transportation systems are well-developed in Japan. Top left: A "bullet" train pulls into Odawa. Bottom: A high-speed freeway cuts through part of downtown Tokyo.

*See Pronunciation Guide.

asking: Has Japan placed too much emphasis on increasing production? Is Japan changing too rapidly? Can valued traditions survive in a modern industrial society?

As a major industrial nation, Japan has yet another problem: The country has very few natural resources. It must import the great bulk of the fuel and raw materials that its industries use. To pay for these imports, Japan must export a vast amount of manufactured goods. It is almost completely dependent on foreign trade for its survival. So far Japan has profited from its trade with the world. The value of its exports has been greater than the cost of its imports. This, however, has created a great deal of envy and resentment among other nations. Some, including the United States, fear the competition of Japanese goods.

The need for understanding. The tensions created by economic rivalry between Japan and other nations is likely to increase in the years ahead. Competition for the world's diminishing supply of fuels and other raw materials could become severe. If conflicts are to be avoided, the great industrial nations must begin to cooperate with each other as never before. Cooperation, of course, requires mutual understanding. As Americans, how well do we understand Japan? At first glance, we might conclude that the Japanese people are very much like us. After all, they have a democratic political system, are highly industrialized, and seem to enjoy "the good life." But in many respects, including politics and business, the Japanese are very different from us. American visitors to Japan quickly become aware of great differences in customs, behavior, beliefs, and values. If the peoples of the United States and Japan are to cooperate in the future for world peace, they will both have to learn much more about each other.

Japan's prosperity keeps Tokyo department stores full of customers and new products.

Double-check

Review

1. Where does Japan rank in total production of goods?

2. What percent of Japanese students graduate from senior high school?

3. List three problems created by the growth of industry in Japan.

4. Where does Japan get the bulk of the fuel and raw materials that its industries use?

5. What will the people of the United States and Japan have to do if they are going to cooperate in the future?

Discussion

1. This chapter provides a brief introductory overview of Japanese society. Did any of the information surprise you? How much do you and your classmates know about Japan as you begin this book? What kinds of things do you hope to learn? How do you think the average Japanese citizen views the average American?

2. What factors determine whether or not a society is "healthy"?

3. Do you believe Japan and other great industrial nations will cooperate to avoid conflicts over the world's diminishing supply of fuels and other raw materials? Why, or why not?

Activities

1. Some students might prepare a large wall map of Japan for use with this book. They could use the map on page 6 as a guide and then add information to it from other maps, including others in later chapters of this book.

2. One word in Chapter 1 is starred (*). This indicates that it is in the Pronunciation Guide at the back of the book. A committee of students might assume primary responsibility for teaching fellow students how to pronounce starred words. They could do this, in advance, for all future chapters.

3. Some students might prepare lists of all the products they can find at school or at home that are "made in Japan." The individual lists could then be combined into a master list which could serve as a stimulus for discussion of how trade between Japan and the U.S. might affect workers and consumers in the two countries.

Skills

TRADE BETWEEN U.S. AND JAPAN

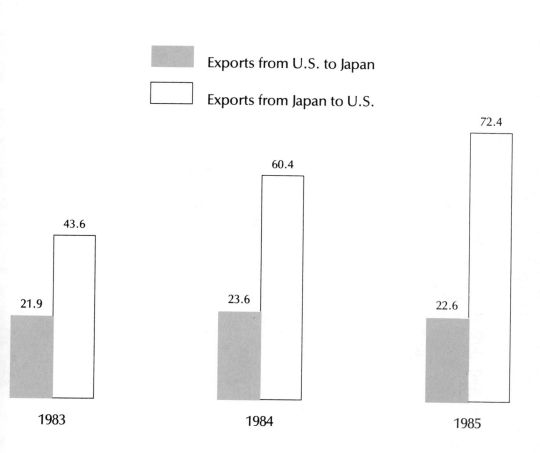

Exports from U.S. to Japan

Exports from Japan to U.S.

(Figures are in billions of dollars)

Source: U.S. Department of Commerce

Use the graph above and information in Chapter 1 to answer the following questions.

1. What is represented by the dark bars? The light bars?

2. What do the numbers above the bars stand for?

3. According to the graph, in what year was trade between Japan and the U.S. the most balanced? The least balanced?

4. During what year did Japan export the most valuable amount to the United States?

5. If trade between the two countries continues at the same rates, which country's dollar value in exports is likely to increase more rapidly? How do you know?

Chapter 2

Geography

Do you think that cities in the United States are crowded? If so, try living in a Japanese city for a while. After that you'll think that our cities are like the "wide open spaces."

In Tokyo you will be overwhelmed by the huge crowds in the downtown streets, shopping centers, and train stations. More than 11 million people — about 10 percent of the entire population of Japan — live within the central city and its suburbs. It may be the heaviest concentration of people in the world. Japan has more than 150 cities with populations of 100,000 or more, and space is in short supply in all of them. Tokyo residents have less than one tenth of the park space that people in New York City have.

Living space for families is unbelievably small. One third of the housing facilities measure an average of 11 feet by 11 feet — about the same size as one room in a U.S. city apartment. This space is usually divided into two tiny rooms for living and sleeping, plus an even tinier kitchen and bathroom.

Japan's commuter trains are very fast and almost always on time, but during rush hours they resemble a mob scene. Normally polite Japanese forget their manners in a mad crush to board them. Station attendants push inside those who are bulging out of the doors.

16

Many people, little space. Why are Japan's cities so terribly overcrowded? A brief look at the area, population, and terrain of the islands that comprise Japan will provide some of the answers.

In size Japan is smaller than France and only slightly larger than Great Britain. In population, however, Japan far exceeds any country of Western Europe. Japan today has about 115 million people, roughly twice that of either France or Great Britain. Among all the nations of the world, Japan's population ranks seventh. The number of people in Japan has more than doubled since 1900, and is still increasing. In recent years, however, the rate of growth has been much smaller. This reflects a trend toward smaller families that began in the late 1950's. If the trend continues, Japan's population should level off at about 135 million by the end of this century.

The amount of living space within Japan is sharply limited by the country's mountainous terrain. More than four fifths of the land is covered with mountains that are quite steep and rugged. Less than one fifth of Japan's surface is level enough to permit farming and most forms of industry. As a result, the bulk of the population is squeezed into the level areas that lie mainly along the seacoasts. The largest level area is the region around Tokyo; most of the others extend down from Tokyo along the Pacific Coast to the Inland Sea (see map, page 23).

The most heavily developed area lies between Tokyo and Osaka,* a distance of 340 miles. It contains one third of Japan's population and is comparable to the "strip city" that runs along the East Coast of the United States from Boston to Washington, D.C.

Japan's mountains make most of the country uninhabitable, but they also give it much of its great natural beauty. Though generally smaller than the mountains of America's West, they are heavily forested and each season produces wondrous changes of color.

18

A gentle climate. Japan's climate is roughly comparable to that of the East Coast of the United States. Its four main islands are, from north to south, Hokkaido,* Honshu,* Shikoku,* and Kyushu.* If you were to superimpose them on a map of our East Coast, they would extend from Maine to Florida. The most densely populated part of Japan, on the island of Honshu, lies on the same latitude as North Carolina. The surrounding oceans, however, tend to make the winters and summers in Japan more moderate than in comparable areas of our East Coast. They also bring more humidity and rain. The rainfall is heaviest from early spring to early autumn. Late autumn and winter are relatively dry, and most of Japan at that time enjoys long stretches of mild, sunny weather.

Rugged terrain makes scenery like this fairly typical along Japanese coastlines.

One exception to this rule is the coast of northern Honshu on the Sea of Japan. Winter winds from Siberia blow across the sea which separates the Japanese islands from the Asiatic mainland. These winds pick up considerable moisture along the way and often dump as much as five to six feet of snow on this part of Honshu. By contrast, the country's Pacific Coast from Tokyo south is warmed by the Japan Current and may be having fairly balmy weather at the same time.

When disasters strike. Moderate temperatures and ample rainfall combine to make most of Japan luxuriantly green eight months a year. In other respects, however, nature has been less kind to the Japanese.

In the late summer and early fall, parts of the country are likely to be struck by typhoons that cause great devastation. Japan also has many active volcanoes, and earthquakes are a daily occurrence. Fortunately, most quakes are mild and cause little damage. But occasionally some are extremely destructive. On September 1, 1923, for example, a severe earthquake struck Tokyo and nearby Yokohama.* The quake and the fires that followed it leveled half of Tokyo, most of Yokohama, and killed about 130,000 people.

The Japanese are accustomed to natural disasters and tend to accept them stoically. They have also shown a great capacity to rebuild after each disaster and start over again.

Small farms, big crops. As already indicated, Japan has very little land that is suitable for farming. Only about 15 percent of the nation's total area is actually used for growing food.

Although land is scarce, Japanese farming is so productive that it provides the population with up to 70 per-

Even southern (top left) and central (bottom) Japan get snow at higher elevations. This is why these farmhouse roofs are so steep.

cent of its food supply. Japanese crop yields per acre are probably the highest in the world. This high productivity from land that is not very fertile is the result of a long growing season, plentiful rainfall, skillful farming techniques, and a great deal of hard work.

Since the end of World War II, Japanese farmers have made increasing use of modern technology, including machinery, chemical fertilizers, and insecticides. The use of machines is limited, however, by the very small size of the farms. In most of Japan, the average farm is only 2.5 acres; and the largest, about 10 acres. Big tractors and combines would be completely impractical in such small areas.

A Japanese tractor is about the same size as an American lawn mower that the driver sits on. Other Japanese farm machines are on an equally small scale. These include cultivators, threshers, and motors to run irrigation pumps.

The use of new technology has greatly reduced the need for farm workers in Japan. Until about 1950, almost half the population of Japan was engaged in agriculture. Today only about 15 percent of the Japanese are farmers, and many of them only part-time.

Most of the young men and many of the young women have gone to live and work in the cities. They may return to the old family farms to help out during very busy seasons, but only temporarily. More and more, Japanese farms are being run by the elderly, or by women whose husbands commute to jobs in nearby cities.

The number-one crop. For those who remain on the farms, the work is quite arduous. Japan's principal crop is rice, which is grown in irrigated fields in almost every part of the country. Irrigated rice cultivation requires the intensive use of human labor. As a rule, one worker is needed for each acre. In the United States,

POPULATION DENSITY

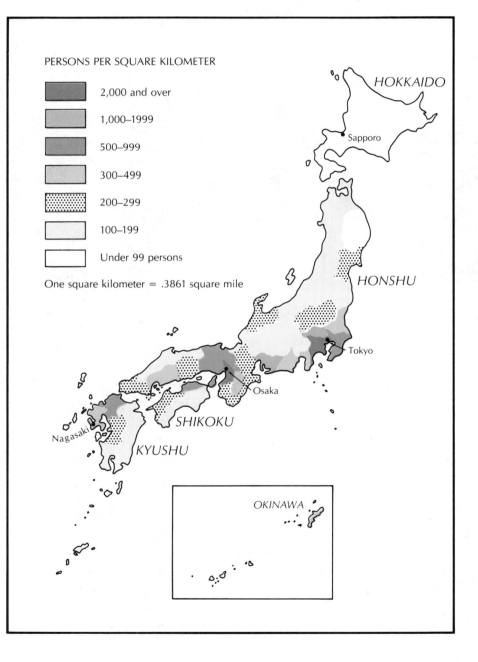

PERSONS PER SQUARE KILOMETER

- 2,000 and over
- 1,000–1999
- 500–999
- 300–499
- 200–299
- 100–199
- Under 99 persons

One square kilometer = .3861 square mile

HOKKAIDO

Sapporo

HONSHU

Tokyo

Osaka

SHIKOKU

Nagasaki

KYUSHU

OKINAWA

Much Japanese farm work is done by women, even the back-breaking job of transplanting rice shoots (above). Right: Woman on Kyushu Island wears a typical farm worker's outfit.

where dry-field farming is practiced, one worker using big machines can cultivate 90 acres. Irrigated rice cultivation may seem inefficient by comparison, but it does have one advantage — it produces much higher yields per acre than dry-field farming. This is important in Japan where there is so little land that can be farmed.

In many parts of Japan, the growing season is long enough to permit two crops of rice to be produced each year. The work begins in April when the seeds are planted close together in muddy soil. After they sprout, the seedlings are transplanted in flooded fields that are surrounded by dikes. Though machines have been developed to transplant rice shoots, many farmers still do it by hand. Stooping down to transplant the shoots is very

24

hard work, and so is the almost constant job of hoeing and weeding that follows. The rice grows gradually until it is several inches above the water. When it ripens, the fields are drained. Then the rice is cut with a hand sickle, tied into small bundles, and dried on poles near the fields. Afterward it is threshed, either by hand with a flail, or with a small machine that is hand-fed. Finally the rice is hulled (removed from its covering shell) and polished. While the work of threshing and polishing is going on, a second crop of rice is being planted that will be harvested in the fall.

Forty percent of Japan's agricultural land is devoted to irrigated rice cultivation, and the rest to dry-field crops of other grains, vegetables, fruit, and tea. Because there is so little land that can be cultivated, farmers often plant vegetables on terraced hillsides or on small plots in mountain valleys. Almost every inch of soil in Japan that can be used to grow food is used.

In the traditional Japanese diet, polished white rice is the staple food. It is eaten in large quantities at all three meals, garnished at times with small portions of vegetables and fish. The importance of rice to the Japanese is conveyed by their word *gohan** which means both "cooked rice" and "meal." Fish is the main source of protein for the Japanese people. Japanese fishing fleets operate everywhere, and their catch is the largest in the world. Much of it is exported. In Japan's coastal waters, which have always been an important food resource, shellfish and vitamin-rich seaweeds are cultivated extensively.

In recent years, the Japanese diet has become more varied. Bread, meat, and dairy products have been gaining favor, while the consumption of rice has been declining. One very noticeable result of this change is that young Japanese today are several inches taller than their parents or grandparents.

Japan Superimposed on the East Coast of the United States

A dependent giant. While Japan's population has increased from 60 million in 1925 to 115 million today, the standard of living has also improved immeasurably. This has been made possible by a big expansion of industry, especially since 1950. As an industrial giant, however, Japan is on shaky ground because it is poor in natural resources. Japan has practically no oil, iron ore, or lead, and little coal, copper, zinc, and other raw materials. It must import all of these vital resources.

27

The danger of this dependence became quite clear late in 1973. At that time, Arab oil-producing nations temporarily halted the sale of petroleum to many countries, including the United States and Japan. Afterward the Arab nations quadrupled the price. Japan, which imports 80 percent of its petroleum from the Middle East, felt especially threatened. Japan's economy weathered that storm. But its rate of growth has since declined from 10 percent a year to six percent, and inflation has become a serious problem.

Japan is equally dependent on foreign trade to pay for its imports of raw materials. Japanese steel, ships, machinery, computers, and a host of consumer goods are sold all over the world. A sharp decrease in the markets for its products because of competition, war, or depression would be disastrous. Japan's dependence on the outside world for raw materials and foreign markets to pay for them is the most basic fact of its economic life today.

Urban-industrial pollution. The concentration of industry in cities inevitably leads to pollution, and Japan is no exception. Partly because its cities are clustered together in a very limited area, Japan has the highest rate of pollution in the world.

Smog — the accumulation of smoke, dust, and fumes dumped into the air by factories and automobile exhausts — is a serious problem. Tokyo dumps twice as many of these pollutants into the air as New York, and its overcast is worse than that of Los Angeles. In *Japanese Society Today,* professor Tadashi Fukutake* of the University of Tokyo writes: "City people are coughing and gasping for breath and complaining of smarting eyes from smog." Japan's coastal waters are also being polluted by the industrial wastes that are poured into them. In 1973 the news that dozens of people had died of mercury poisoning after eating contaminated shellfish caused a nationwide panic. Cities and factories are not the only

28

These Tokyo residents marched with banners and breathing masks to demonstrate their concern over Japan's urban air pollution.

polluters. The increasing use of chemical fertilizers and insecticides by Japanese farmers has contaminated many rivers and streams.

Many Japanese are also disturbed by the large-scale destruction of trees in mountain areas for roads and recreational facilities to attract tourists. Others are upset by the huge traffic snarls and noise caused by the increased use of cars. And some complain that the new high-rise office buildings going up in Tokyo and other cities deprive them of their "right to sunshine."

As the Japanese see the great natural beauty and peace of their land being spoiled, more and more are questioning the wisdom of ever-increasing industrial production. They wonder: "Have we paid too high a price for industrialization and prosperity? What can be done about our overcrowded cities and pollution?"

Double-check

Review

1. Where does Japan's population rank among all nations of the world?

2. What geographic feature limits the amount of living space in Japan?

3. With which part of the United States is Japan's climate roughly comparable?

4. List four factors that contribute to Japan's high productivity from land that is not very fertile.

5. How does Japan's pollution rate compare with the rest of the world?

Discussion

1. Most Japanese cities are extremely crowded, and living space in many is almost unbelievably small. Would living in such conditions bother you? Why, or why not? How do you think Japanese citizens might react to the vast spaces in parts of the United States? Would you prefer rural or city life in Japan? Why?

2. Because of typhoons, volcanoes, and earthquakes, many Japanese people have learned to deal with natural disasters. How do you think the members of your community would respond to such events?

3. This chapter discusses several ways in which the geographical features of Japan affect the lives of people who live there. Would it make sense to say, "Geography is destiny"? Why, or why not?

Activities

1. If there is a Japanese restaurant in or near your community, some students might eat there and then describe what they ate to the rest of the class. They might bring a menu back with them. Other students might bring Japanese cookbooks to class for display and discussion. Still others might prepare some traditional Japanese dishes and share them in class.

2. The shortage of living space in Tokyo might be dramatized in your classroom by measuring a space 11 feet long and 11 feet wide on the floor. Then some students could try to divide this area into the four rooms described in the chapter — with a minimum of furniture.

3. A bulletin board display of photos and drawings depicting both the natural beauty and the pollution of Japan might be assembled from old magazines and newspapers. Some students might draw political cartoons dealing with some of the social problems caused by the crowded and polluted conditions of Japanese urban areas.

Skills

JAPAN'S SOURCES OF ENERGY

1976   **1983**

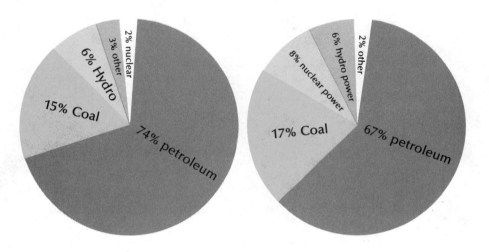

Source: The Japanese Trade Center

Use the pie graphs above and information from the chapter to answer the following questions.

1. What do the graphs above show? Why are there two of them?

2. What is the source of information in the graphs?

3. On which energy sources was Japan more dependent in 1983?

4. On which energy source was Japan less dependent in 1983?

5. Why is Japan decreasing its dependence on petroleum? What event influenced them in this matter?

2
TRADITIONAL
JAPAN

Chapter 3

Early History

WHO WERE THE FIRST PEOPLE to inhabit Japan? Where did they come from, and when? Unfortunately, not very much is known about the origins of the Japanese people. For a long time it was believed that the first humans did not arrive in Japan until about 8000 B.C. This estimate was based on discoveries of early human skeletons along with tools and pottery that indicated a fairly advanced culture. Since the late 1940's, however, the rough tools of a much more primitive culture have been found. Although no complete skeletons have been found with them, the tools clearly belong to a Stone Age people who existed hundreds of thousands of years ago. It is possible that these people came to Japan at a remote time when it was still connected to the Asian continent by land.

Early inhabitants. The human skeletons dating from about 8000 B.C. are of a people closely related to the Chinese and Koreans. Most of these early inhabitants probably came to Japan over a long period of time from northeastern Asia. There is evidence that many crossed over from the Korean peninsula, the closest point

Some Jomon ("rope-marked") pottery has
been traced to ancient Ainu culture in northern
Japan — created, perhaps, by ancestors of this
20th-century Ainu husband and wife.

on the mainland to Japan. Yet some early Japanese may have come from as far away as the South Pacific by a process of "island-hopping." This theory is based in part on the strong similarity between certain Japanese myths and those of various South Pacific island countries.

One thing is certain: The various migrations to Japan halted by the fifth century A.D. From that time until the present, there has been no migration of any consequence into the Japanese islands. The Japanese people "jelled" more than a thousand years ago into a very homogeneous group with very few racial or ethnic minorities.

Perhaps the most distinctive minority group in Japan today are the Ainu.* These people generally differ in appearance from other Japanese, especially in their abundance of facial and body hair. Most of them have been assimilated by the main population. Today fewer than 20,000 Ainu survive as a distinct cultural group on the northern island of Hokkaido.

The Japanese tend to think of themselves as a racially "pure" people comprising a single great family. They seldom accept "foreigners" as full members of their society. This very strong sense of cultural unity was heightened by Japan's relative isolation as an island country for many centuries. In fact, for more than 200 years, from 1638 to 1853, Japan's rulers cut off practically all contacts between their country and the rest of the world.

Of gods and goddesses. While students of Japan are uncertain about the country's beginnings, Japanese mythology is not. According to ancient Japanese stories, Japan and its people were created in this way:

Brother and sister gods Izanagi* and Izanami* were commissioned in heaven to produce a "drifting land." Izanagi thrust his spear into the ocean and, as he withdrew it, a small island was formed. The brother and sister gods then descended to the island by a bridge from heaven. Soon they produced all the Japanese islands, plus a large number of nature gods. Among them were the gods of the sea, the rivers, the woods, the mountains, and the wind.

As Izanagi cleansed and purified himself in a river, he produced many other gods, including the sun goddess, Amaterasu.* She sprang into being as Izanagi washed his left eye. The sun goddess became the ruler of heaven. She then ordered her grandson, Ninigi,* to descend from heaven and establish the rule of his family on earth. She gave him three sacred objects — a mirror, a long sword, and a curved jewel — as symbols of his authority. Ninigi's grandson, Jimmu,* according to mythology, became the first emperor of Japan in 660 B.C.

While these tales are obviously based on the imaginations of people who lived a long time ago, they tell us a great deal about enduring Japanese traditions. Along with other myths, they comprise the "scriptures" of *Shinto,** Japan's oldest native faith. It centers on the worship of nature gods known as *kami.** Shinto, or "the way of the gods," is not a religion that stresses personal ethics. It does not hold men and women responsible for their sins. Rather, it inspires a sense of awe for the wonders of nature and stresses the value of purification rites.

The purification rite is performed by Shinto priests who sprinkle water with a wand. The belief in purification by water has contributed to the Japanese people's great love of bathing and cleanliness.

Today Japan has tens of thousands of Shinto shrines, often in places of great natural beauty. The Japanese also celebrate Shinto festivals with enthusiasm.

The land of "Wa." While very little exact information exists about early Japan, historians have been able to fit the bits and pieces together to form a fairly clear picture. Some information comes from Chinese histories written in the first three centuries A.D.

36

Above: a statue of one of the seven Shinto gods of luck. Below: A Shinto priest leads a ceremony at the sacred shrine at Ise.

The Chinese histories depict Japan, which they called the land of "Wa,*" as a farming and fishing society whose people were divided into a number of tribes. The tribes were ruled by shamans, or priests, who supposedly possessed magical powers. Most of these shamans were women. Here is how one Chinese history describes a queen named Pimiko,* who ruled a large area of Wa:

"Pimiko occupied herself with magic and sorcery, bewitching the people. Though mature in age, she remained unmarried. She had a younger brother who assisted her in ruling the country. After she became the ruler, there were few who saw her. She had 1,000 women as attendants, but only one man. He served her food and drink, and acted as a medium of communication. She resided in a palace surrounded by towers and stockades, with armed guards."

Pimiko was depicted as a mediator between the people and their gods, a role that later became the most sacred function of Japan's emperors and empresses. The Chinese histories described still other Japanese traditions that have persisted to this day. The Japanese showed deference to their superiors by squatting or kneeling with both hands on the ground. They clapped their hands in worship. And they placed great value on ritual cleansing, or purification.

The evidence of the tombs. Knowledge of early Japan also comes from a large number of burial mounds, or tombs, scattered about the country. These tombs characteristically were shaped in the form of keyholes. Although some of them are small, others are huge and must have required an enormous amount of human labor to build. One such mound covers an area of about 80 acres. These tombs were constructed in the fourth to sixth centuries A.D. Clay statues, including those of armored warriors and horses, were found outside the tombs. Inside were found bronze and iron weapons, and tools.

The evidence of these tombs indicates that at this time Japan's tribes were ruled by a nobility of mounted warriors. Where these warriors came from is something of a mystery. Before the fourth century, there is no evidence of horses being used, or even existing, in Japan. One possibility is that these warriors crossed over from Korea and soon took control of the country with their superior military technology. Other objects found in the tombs include the three sacred symbols of authority mentioned in Japanese mythology — a mirror, a long sword, and a curved jewel.

Clay statues and bronze mirrors like these help historians learn about life in Japan between the fourth and sixth centuries.

Tombs found near the present-day cities of Nara* and Osaka have traditionally been identified as those of the first Japanese emperors. These emperors said that they were descended from the sun goddess, the supreme kami of the Shinto faith. Therefore they were entitled to leadership over lesser tribal chiefs. Since their tombs date from after 300 A.D., Japanese mythology's version that the first emperor began his reign in 660 B.C. is obviously false. The present-day emperor of Japan, Hirohito,* is descended from a family that seems to date from at least the early sixth century A.D. This is undoubtedly the longest-reigning family in the world.

How much is known about those whom the warrior nobility ruled? Since about 300 B.C., the mass of Japanese people had been living in permanent farming villages, where they engaged in irrigated rice cultivation. A settled agricultural society stresses obedience to people of higher authority. Children must obey parents, younger brothers must obey older ones, the lowly must obey those of superior status. Irrigated rice cultivation also requires close cooperation in the tending of fields. As Japanese farms were — and still are — family affairs, this need helped develop strong family loyalties. The traditions of obedience to authority and tightly knit families, which took root so long ago, have also endured throughout Japanese history to modern times.

The influence of China. Chinese historians of the first three centuries A.D. viewed Chinese civilization as much further advanced than that of the Japanese. Under the T'ang dynasty emperors (618–907), China became the richest and most powerful country in the world with cities, palaces, and arts that were truly dazzling.

Japan in the seventh century couldn't boast of a good-sized town, not to mention a city. Undoubtedly, Japanese envoys and traders who traveled to China brought back many tales of its splendor. In any event, the Japanese apparently decided that they could learn a great deal from Chinese culture. They began to borrow heavily from its arts, technology, and political and social skills. The object was to make Japan a small replica of China. By the 10th century, Japan had been transformed from a backward, tribal country into an advanced society. This society, however, was not a slavish imitation of China. It was instead a unique new culture that blended China's influences with Japan's own native traditions.

Starting in the sixth century, Japan borrowed from China in the following ways:

1. Religion. Buddhism,* the principal religion of China at this time, was officially introduced to the imperial Japanese court in the year 552. (This court was located in the province of Yamato,* near the present-day cities of Nara and Osaka.) Buddhism gradually began to win favor in court circles, where it tended to replace Shinto.

In spirit Buddhism is quite unlike Shinto. Japan's native religion expresses a love of nature and its forces of reproduction. It is a joyous faith. Buddhism, by contrast, takes a pessimistic view of life in this world. Suffering, it says, is caused by human desires and acquisitiveness. All people are born and reborn many times, prolonging the pain of existence. How can people escape the cycle of rebirths and misery? When they learn to overcome their desires for things that cannot satisfy them and learn to "do right," they will achieve *nirvana,* or enlightenment. Nirvana is a state of mind in which people are above life's trials and become one with the universe. They lose their identities much as a drop of water loses its identity when it merges with the ocean. For most people, however, such release from suffering does not come easily.

Because of its complexity, Buddhism at this time made little headway among Japan's peasant masses. Those who were drawn to Buddhism came mainly from the nobility.

時　小　此　雅　衆　華　瀰　華　病　視　聽　壇　廣　咅　來
王　時　決　音　昌　音　香　鳥　普　狂　惡　皆　門　不　踊
即　諸　雅　有　繢　繢　鳳　鷹　皆　者　者　悉　下　敢　門

Top left: Eighth-century Japanese scrolls (with Chinese writing) tell of previous lives of Buddha. Bottom: 13th-century wood statue with Chinese robes, Japanese hairstyle. Right: ninth-century statue of Shinto goddess. All show Chinese influence on early Japanese culture.

In the 12th century, however, new Buddhist sects arose that became very popular. They preached that nirvana was a paradise where the souls of good people went to enjoy eternal bliss. The wicked were consigned to numerous hells. In this respect, the new Buddhist sects resembled Western Christianity much more than they did the original Buddhism. Moreover, they made the attainment of salvation quite easy. All one had to do was call on the name of Amida Buddha.* This act of faith assured one of entering paradise.

Among Japan's peasant masses, the new Buddhism had a great appeal, but it did not replace Shinto. Instead the two religions existed almost side by side. Buddhism adopted many of the principal gods of Shinto as Buddhist deities, and Shinto shrines were even merged with Buddhist temples. Today most Japanese consider themselves both Shintoists and Buddhists, and see no conflict in having two religions. In fact, Shinto and Buddhism seem to complement each other very well. Such joyous events as birth and marriage are celebrated with Shinto rites. Funerals and communion with the dead are observed with Buddhist rites.

*The ancient statue of the Great Buddha in
the temple of Todaiji remains impressive.*

2. *The arts and sciences.* Buddhism brought to Japan
more than a vigorous new faith. It was a great civilizing
force, introducing to the Japanese the arts and sciences
of China. Japanese converts to Buddhism took the dangerous sea voyage to China to study. After many years,
they would return home as skilled painters, musicians,
poets, and craftsmen.

The imperial court supported magnificent Buddhist temples that housed religious statues and paintings of rare beauty. The most celebrated of these statues, the Great Buddha in the temple of Todaiji,* was 53 feet high and required more than 1,500 tons of copper, tin, and lead, plus 15,000 pounds of gold covering. When the Great Buddha was unveiled in 752, it was truly an "eye-opening" ceremony, for the huge figure was symbolically given life by having the pupils of its eyes filled in. Some 10,000 Buddhist priests attended the ceremony, as well as many visitors from China, India, and other distant lands. It was one of the grandest moments in early Japanese history.

3. Writing. In art, the influence of Chinese teachers on Japan was all for the good. In the realm of writing, however, borrowing from China led to serious and long-lasting problems. The Japanese had never devised a writing system of their own. Instead they attempted to adapt Chinese written characters to express their own spoken language. While this effort gave the Japanese a written language for the first time, it created difficulties that still plague them today:

• In the Chinese system, each written symbol or character stands for a separate word. Chinese students, and later the Japanese, had to memorize thousands of such characters before they could be considered literate. Students are still burdened by this laborious process.

• The spoken language of Japanese is as different from Chinese as it is from English. By using Chinese characters to express their native speech, the Japanese were trying to fit a square peg into a round hole.

In the ninth century, the Japanese devised a more efficient system for recording their language. It is a mixture of Chinese characters standing for words and about 50 symbols (derived from Chinese characters) that stand for sounds. These phonetic symbols are called *kana.**

This stylized portrait of Prince Shotoku
and his sons was painted after his death.
Note scepter of royal authority in his hand.

Although this hybrid system made it easier for the Japanese to adapt Chinese writing, it remains without doubt the most complex written language in the world today.

4. *Government.* The rulers of the province of Yamato claimed descent from the sun goddess, and therefore the right to rule all of Japan. In reality their authority over distant provinces was quite limited. China, by contrast, was a highly unified state whose emperors were all-powerful. Since Japan was borrowing so much from Chinese culture, it seemed logical to some Japanese that they should emulate China's system of government as well.

Powerful Japanese political figures like Crown Prince Shotoku* (574–622) sought to establish the rulers of the Yamato state as emperors with all the power and majesty of the Chinese monarchs. Shotoku expressed this concept in a message that he addressed to the Chinese emperor in 607 on behalf of the reigning empress of Japan. It began, "From the sovereign of the Land of the Rising Sun [Japan] to the sovereign of the Land of the Setting Sun [China]." This salutation was not appreciated by the Chinese emperor, who regarded the Japanese as upstart barbarians. But it indicated that Shotoku and other Japanese leaders already envisioned their emperor as the equal of China's. Shotoku is also celebrated in Japanese history because he was an early champion of Buddhism and sent the first missions of envoys, students, Buddhist monks, and translators to study in China.

In 645 the imperial court adopted the name of *Nihon,** or *Nippon,* for the nation. It literally means "source of the sun," and probably was inspired by the phrase "Land of the Rising Sun" that Shotoku had used in his message to the Chinese emperor. The Chinese pronunciation for Nihon was "Jihpen.*" This pronunciation was introduced to Europe in the 13th century by Marco Polo, the Venetian traveler who spent many years in China. It entered the English vocabulary as *Japan.*

*When the Japanese imperial court moved
from the city of Nara, it settled in Heian,
which became Kyoto. Parts of this
ancient city are shown in this painting.*

5. *Cities.* If the Japanese emperors were to rival those
of China, they had to have an imposing capital city modeled after the Chinese. Until this time, the imperial court
had moved from one location to another, and Japan had
no cities at all. In 708 construction of a capital was begun
at the site of Nara. When the capital was completed two
years later, Nara contained wide avenues and impressive
palaces, residences, and Buddhist temples. Some of
these temples still stand today and are among the oldest
wooden buildings in the world. Later in the century, the
court built a new capital 30 miles to the north at a site
called Heian.* It remained the capital of the imperial
family until 1868 and is now the modern city of Kyoto.*

48

One reason for the move to Kyoto was a scandal that involved a Buddhist priest with the reigning Empress Shotoku. Using his influence over the empress, the priest rose to a position of great power and planned to take over the throne itself. The court was so shocked by this conspiracy that it decided to get away from Nara and the presence of its many Buddhist temples and priests. It also apparently decided that in the future women would no longer be allowed to succeed to the throne. There have been only two exceptions to the rule since that time.

Court aristocrats take power. The Japanese throne was troubled by more than a Buddhist priest. Its power was being undermined by members of the court nobility. By the middle of the ninth century the emperors were reduced to the status of political figureheads who reigned, but did not rule. How did this come about?

Japan's leaders had tried to create a strong central government modeled after China's. Under the emperor, they established many government ministries and bureaus to administer the entire country. In China, however, most high government posts were filled by qualified civil servants who had passed examinations. The Japanese admired the examination system, but did not emulate it. Instead high government posts came to be inherited more and more by noble families at the court. These families used their positions to increase their large private estates, which generally were tax-free. As these estates grew, the income of the imperial government from land taxes shrank steadily, until it could no longer function effectively. Power became concentrated in the hands of great landowning court aristocrats.

The wealthiest and most powerful of these aristocrats were the members of the Fujiwara* family. By the second half of the ninth century, they controlled the throne completely. Their favorite technique of control was to

This sketch depicts Fujiwara-No-Kamatari, founder of the Fujiwara clan in the seventh century. Note the scepter of authority.

marry a Fujiwara girl to a young emperor. After the girl had borne him a son, the emperor would be persuaded to retire, sometimes to the peace and quiet of a Buddhist monastery. Then the head of the Fujiwara family would act as regent for the child emperor. In time the Fujiwara family took over almost every high office at the court. Japan's emperors retained their role as leaders of the Shinto religion. But with few exceptions, they have been politically powerless for the last 1,000 years.

50

A native culture flourishes. At the same time that the Fujiwara were taking power, Japan stopped sending missions of envoys, students, and priests to China. The Japanese no longer felt that they needed to take lessons from the Chinese. They believed that they were sufficiently advanced to develop their arts independently, and this they did with considerable flair and enthusiasm. During the age of the Fujiwara (866–1160), Japanese poetry and prose were especially creative. Using the new kana symbols that made it easier to write Japanese, members of the court avidly composed poems, kept diaries, and produced the world's first novel, *The Tale of Genji*.

With her writing scrolls stacked on shelves, Murasaki Shikibu, authoress of the world's first novel, takes a nap in this sketch.

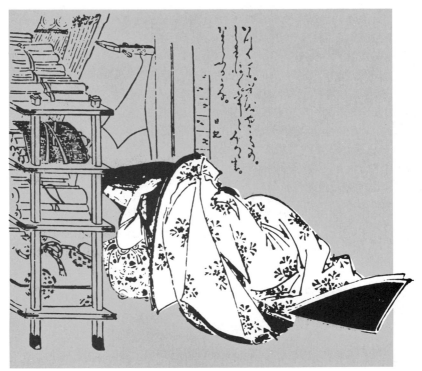

The Japanese were particularly fond of writing short poems, called *tanka*,* that contained exactly 31 syllables each. Why they preferred brief poetry is uncertain, but their language may have had something to do with it. Most Japanese words end in vowels, which makes rhyme easy — perhaps *too* easy and a little monotonous. So the Japanese concentrated on short five-line poems that, during the Fujiwara period, evoked rather gentle emotions. The following poem, written by a member of the Kyoto court, is typical:

> *This perfectly still*
> *Spring day bathed in the soft light*
> *From the spread-out sky,*
> *Why do the cherry blossoms*
> *So restlessly scatter down?*

The aristocratic members of the Kyoto court were far removed from the everyday concerns of Japan's peasant masses. They had very little to do except devote themselves to the arts of music and poetry, to fashions and perfumes, to walks in gardens, and to the pursuit of love affairs. Their ideals were refinement, good manners, and good taste. The lives of these aristocrats were described by Murasaki Shikibu,* a lady-in-waiting at the court, in *The Tale of Genji.* Written around the year 1000, it is still considered a literary masterpiece. Its leading character, Genji, is an emperor's son who possesses all the qualities admired by the Kyoto courtiers. He is exceptionally handsome; a "ladies' man"; and a skilled poet, musician, dancer, and calligrapher (a handwriting artist). Above all, he has perfect taste. Halfway through the book, Genji dies, and the rest of the novel is permeated with sadness and a sense of insecurity. Did Lady Murasaki suspect that the refined, peaceful society of aristocratic Japan was doomed and would soon give way to the rule of rough fighting men?

Double-check

Review

1. When did the various migrations of consequence into the Japanese islands end?

2. What is Japan's oldest native faith and on what is it centered?

3. List five aspects of Japanese society that were borrowed from China, starting in the sixth century.

4. What does the Japanese word *nippon* mean when translated into English?

5. What was the world's first novel? When was it written?

Discussion

1. This chapter briefly describes a Japanese myth about the origin of Japan and its people. Can such myths contain truths even if the events they describe might not have happened? What does this story suggest about Japanese attitudes toward the forces of nature and the relationship of humans to those forces? What might be the significance of the three sacred objects?

2. Most Japanese consider themselves both Shintoists and Buddhists. Does this seem contradictory or logical? Do people in the U.S. ever combine religious beliefs in a similar way? Explain your answers.

3. What are the various sources of evidence for drawing conclusions about early Japanese history? Which of these sources do you believe are the most reliable? The least reliable? Why?

Activities

1. Several student committees might be formed to research and report to the rest of the class on some of the following topics: Other Civilizations' Creation Myths; The Latest Findings and Theories About the Origins of Japan's First Inhabitants; Shinto Beliefs and Practices; Buddhist Beliefs and Practices in Japan; The First Japanese Emperors; the Fujiwara Family; The Ainu Culture; The Japanese Written Language.

2. Some students might read parts of *The Tale of Genji* and prepare oral or written reports on the material, emphasizing what readers can learn about life in early Japan from the novel.

3. Two or more students might role-play an imaginary meeting between Japan's Crown Prince Shotoku and the Chinese emperor in 607 A.D. The meeting might be humorous or serious — or a mixture of both.

Skills

Readers' Guide to Periodical Literature

March 1976–February 1977

Page 577

SHINTO
Emperor: still god to some. N.L. Kennedy. Chr Today 20:41 My 7 '76
Shinto: a secret world; exhibition. K. Kuh. il Sat R 4:74-6 D 11 '76
Shinto strides; rites of the *omoto* sect at New York's Cathedral of St. John the Divine Episcopal. N.L. Kennedy. Chr Today 20:43-4 My 21 '76

Page 995

JAPAN — *Continued*
Religious institutions and affairs
Praying for death; elderly worshipers seeking good deaths. B. Krisher. il por Newsweek 87:10 F 16 '76
Word in Japan. N. L. Kennedy. Chr Today 21:77-8 N 5 '76
see also
Baptists in Japan
Shinto

Abbreviations:

D — December

F — February

My — May

N — November

il — illustrated

por — portrait

Chr Today — *Christianity Today*

Sat R — *Saturday Review*

Use the above listings from Readers' Guide to Periodical Literature *and information in Chapter 3 to answer the following questions.*

1. In what type of publications can you find the articles listed in *Readers' Guide?*
   (a) books   (b) magazines   (c) newspapers

2. How many articles about the Shinto religion are listed in this edition of *Readers' Guide?*
   (a) six   (b) two   (c) three

3. Which of the magazines listed above is the one most likely to have pictures of Japanese people in it?
   (a) *Christianity Today*   (b) *Saturday Review*   (c) *Newsweek*

4. Under which major heading would you find articles about Baptists in Japan?
   (a) Religion   (b) Baptists   (c) Japan

5. Judging from the above articles' titles (and using information in Chapter 3), in which magazine is the article that is most likely to mention Buddhism?
   (a) *Christianity Today*   (b) *Saturday Review*   (c) *Newsweek*

Chapter 4

Feudalism

WHILE THE COURT ARISTOCRATS at Kyoto were devoting themselves to the gentler arts, a growing number of men in the provinces were cultivating the arts of war. The decline in the power of the central government spurred provincial leaders to form vigilante bands of warriors to protect themselves against marauders and other local enemies. Once again fighting men on horseback began to take control of the land, as others had done centuries before. By the 12th century the most powerful of these provincial warrior bands were fighting each other for supremacy, and the court nobility as well as the emperors were helpless. In 1185 Minamoto Yoritomo,* the commander-in-chief of warrior bands in the eastern provinces, defeated his rivals for power and established a military government to rule Japan.

The first shogun. Yoritomo made no attempt to depose either the emperor or the Fujiwara. The tradition of imperial rule, though now only a fiction, was one that even he had to respect. The only title that Yoritomo took was that of shogun,* meaning generalissimo or top commander, of the emperor's army. The title was given to him by the emperor himself. But while Yoritomo left the sham government at Kyoto intact, he set up his own government, called the shogunate,* at Kamakura* near present-day Tokyo.

Yoritomo rewarded his loyal followers by appointing them to positions of authority in the provinces. Usually they became local military governors or the managers of estates, and collected taxes from the peasants who tilled the soil. Yoritomo further agreed to protect them from any enemies who might threaten them. This simple political system, which is based almost entirely on personal ties of loyalty and service, is known as feudalism. It lasted almost 700 years in Japan, until 1868. During that time, Japan was ruled continuously by a class of warrior aristocrats and their retainers.

The samurai code. Feudal relationships in Japan were similar to those that existed in Europe during the Middle Ages between lords and vassals, or knights. Japanese knights were called samurai* — those who "served." They had an unwritten code of behavior that later came to be known as bushido* — "the way of the warrior." The samurai code emphasized unswerving loyalty to one's overlord, and family solidarity. It placed great value on courage, honor, self-discipline, and complete indifference to suffering or death. The warrior held his own life lightly and was prepared to die unflinchingly in battle. Capture or surrender was considered dishonorable.

Rather than fall into enemy hands, samurai commonly

Top right: 700-year-old wood sculpture of Minamoto Yoritomo. Bottom: painting of battle between two clans.

速被法

Top, far left: 18th-century samurai armor.
Near: Samurai quickly gets into armor kept ready on
hanger. Bottom: Modern-day festival honors samurai.
Above: 14th-century Himeji Castle, near Kobe.

took their own lives in an act called *harakiri** or *seppuku*.* (Harakiri means "belly-slitting." Seppuku, a more formal expression, means "disembowelment.") This act was performed by stabbing a knife into the left side of the abdomen, drawing it across to the right, and giving a final upward twist toward the chest. Samurai committed suicide in this fashion not only to avoid capture, but to atone for any unworthy behavior.

Loyalty, samurai-style. The code of bushido is best illustrated by a story that is still extremely popular in Japan. Based on a true incident, it has been dramatized countless times on the stage as *A Treasury of Loyal Hearts*. Japanese audiences see it as a classic example of noble conduct that has not lost its meaning. The story is as follows:

In 1701 a feudal lord became enraged when he was insulted by a high official of the shogun's government. Drawing his sword, he attacked the official and wounded him. This offense was punishable by death, and the shogun's government ordered the warrior aristocrat to commit suicide by disembowelment. (At this time, seppuku was the usual sentence given members of the warrior class who committed serious crimes.)

The lord's samurai followers were appalled. For now they had become *ronin** (samurai without a master) and had lost their place in society. Forty-seven of them swore to avenge their master's death. Aware that the government would be watching them, they bided their time for two years. Then, on a cold winter night, they broke into the home of their master's old enemy and killed him. After placing his head on their master's grave, they surrendered to the authorities.

The Japanese people hailed the 47 ronin for their act of loyalty, and the ronin soon became national heroes. Even among the shogun's officials there were many who wished to drop all charges against them. However, the shogun's laws had been violated, and the men had to be punished. Finally, after months of debate, they were ordered to disembowel themselves. Buried side by side in a Tokyo temple, they achieved an immortality matched by few others in Japan's history.

Since the end of World War II, the practice of suicide by disembowelment has become rare in Japan. But other features of the feudal warrior's code still influence the Japanese today. Among them are a strong sense of duty and self-discipline, and a great capacity for personal loyalty.

Japan's samurai were extremely proud of their horseback-riding ability, as well as their skill with the bow and arrow. Later a curved sword became one of their principal weapons and a symbol of their status. As recently as

World War II, Japanese officers wore these swords even though they were completely impractical as weapons.

The Mongol invaders. Samurai bands usually fought one another, but on two occasions they were called upon to repel a foreign invader. In the 13th century, one of the greatest military powers the world had ever known, the Mongols, began a campaign of conquest. Led at first by Ghengis Khan, the Mongols swept over most of Asia and large areas of eastern Europe. By 1270 they were eyeing the Japanese islands. Their leader at this time, Kublai Khan, sent envoys to Japan demanding that the country pay tribute to him. The terrified courtiers at Kyoto were quite ready to yield, but the shogun's government at Kamakura sharply rejected the khan's envoys.

Mongol bowmen battle a Japanese samurai
— while a gunpowder bomb bursts in air —
in this picture scroll painted around 1293.

The khan was outraged, of course, and began making preparations to invade and conquer Japan. In 1274 a Mongol force of 40,000 men set sail from Korea and landed in northern Kyushu. Their weapons included gunpowder bombs that were hurled by catapults. The Japanese samurai resisted stoutly but were no match for the Mongols. That night, however, a typhoon struck the coast and destroyed much of the Mongol armada. The Mongols were forced to abandon their invasion.

The Japanese knew that the Mongols would return and prepared for it. They built a wall to protect their coast, where the first army had landed, and a fleet of small, fast ships to harass the Mongol troop transports.

The Mongols landed in 1281 with 150,000 men, the largest overseas invasion force ever assembled up to that time. Though heavily outnumbered, the samurai fought stubbornly for two months and held the Mongols in check. Then another typhoon struck, forcing the Mongols back to their ships and blowing them out to sea. Many of the ships were destroyed, and once again the invaders had to turn back to the mainland.

To the Japanese, the typhoons were the "divine winds," or *kamikaze*,* that had been unleashed by the gods to protect their sacred land. A tradition developed that, in times of peril, Japan would always be saved from destruction by the intervention of the gods. Japan was not faced with an invasion again until the last months of World War II. In 1945 Japanese suicide pilots who then volunteered to dive their bombers onto U.S. Navy ships were regarded as the embodiment of the "divine winds," and were called kamikaze.

Feudal government in Japan had begun successfully with the establishment of a military regime by Yoritomo at Kamakura. By the late 13th century, however, the authority of the Kamakura shogunate over local feudal lords began to erode. In 1331 Japan was torn by an internal revolt, and a few years later the shogunate at Kamakura was destroyed. A new family of shoguns, the Ashikaga,* was established at Kyoto in 1338. From time to time, the Ashikaga succeeded in restoring a measure of peace and unity to Japan. But their control over local feudal lords was never as effective as that of the earlier Kamakura shoguns. By the late 15th century, the power of the Ashikaga disintegrated completely, and local strong men reigned supreme.

The influence of Zen. Despite the growing disorders and disunity, the country continued to make great strides culturally. While Japan's peasants were embracing new Buddhist sects that promised easy salvation, many samurai were also being drawn to a different sort of Buddhism — Zen.* Zen, which literally means "meditation," was introduced to Japan from China about the time Yoritomo took power as shogun.

In Zen, enlightenment is sought by lengthy meditation while sitting in a cross-legged position. This is a process that requires extreme mental and physical self-discipline. The student of Zen is asked to solve problems, known as *koan,** that seem nonsensical. What, for example, is the nature of the sound made by clapping with one hand instead of two? The object of the question is not to find a logical answer, but to induce meditation that will lead to greater self-understanding.

For the samurai leaders of Japan's feudal age, Zen had a strong attraction. Its rigorous self-discipline was admired by fighting men whose own code of bushido emphasized mental and physical toughness.

Japan's shoguns and other feudal lords supported Zen monasteries. And they became the nation's chief havens of cultural activity amid the growing turbulence of the times. Like the Buddhist converts of an earlier age, Zen monks studied in China and mastered its most advanced arts. They applied to these arts their own beliefs in sim-

63

plicity and restraint to produce styles that became characteristically Japanese. Among the art forms that were strongly influenced by Zen monks and still flourish in Japan today are the following:

1. *Tea ceremony*. The formal art of serving tea is aimed at creating a beautiful experience. In its traditional form, the tea ceremony takes place in a small room whose furnishings are severely simple. Its entrance is so low that the guests must crawl through it on their hands and knees. This act symbolizes their humility and acceptance (at least temporarily) of social equality. The mood that the tea ceremony seeks is one of complete spiritual calm and detachment from worldly concerns. The guests silently observe the slow, deliberate movements of the host as he prepares and serves the tea. After the ceremony has been completed, conversation is usually limited to a few comments about the beauty of the pottery. The pottery may be rough and cracked, but by Zen standards it is beautiful.

2. *Landscape gardening*. Japanese gardens are intended to produce a feeling of unity with nature. Within an area that is usually very limited, they seek to create a miniature replica of great mountains, forests, and bodies of water. This is accomplished by the artful arrangement of a few rocks, small bushes and trees, and a pond or stream. Some Japanese gardens are purely symbolic and contain no plants at all. A world-famous garden in Kyoto, for example, consists solely of white sand that is carefully raked to represent ocean waves, and a number of rocks that suggest islands jutting out of the sea. This "dry garden" is about the size of a tennis court. It fascinates Japanese and foreign tourists alike, creating for many of them an image of a majestic seascape.

This modern-day tea ceremony is being prepared by a trained Japanese geisha.

3. Flower arrangement. A few flowers, Zen masters said, could capture the essence of many by drawing on the imagination of the viewer. With the addition of a few leaves, for example, one or two gracefully arranged flowers suggest more than several large bouquets. Today most well-bred Japanese girls are trained in this art.

4. Landscape painting in ink. The belief that a little can suggest a lot is also expressed by Zen artists in their paintings of nature scenes. With a few bold strokes of black India ink, the artists often convey the grandeur of rugged mountains, forests, and waterfalls more vividly than paintings that are full of color and details. In these one-color landscapes, human beings appear as insignificant, antlike figures engulfed in the vastness of the universe.

All of these arts have a number of things in common. They emphasize simplicity, essentials, and a deep love of nature. At the court of the shogunate, which moved to Kyoto in the 14th century, the warrior aristocrats were entertained by a different kind of art. This was *No** theater, a highly stylized form of drama that combined music, dance, and poetry. Although the stage itself was bare, the actors wore costumes of gold brocade and other bright colors. Some wore masks that seemed to express emotion as movingly as any human face. Symbolic rather than realistic, No drama usually dealt with remote or supernatural events. Elegant and mysterious, it suited the more refined tastes of the feudal lords at the shogun's court. It is still performed today by acting groups dedicated to the art.

Top left: A monk carefully rakes a "dry garden" in Tokyo; bottom: a stylized landscape, painted by a monk. Both show Zen influence on Japanese culture.

From disorder to unity. In the late 15th century civil warfare spread throughout Japan as the power of the Ashikaga shoguns disintegrated. Local feudal lords became masters within their domains and ruled like kings. During the next century the stronger lords gradually swallowed up the domains of the weaker ones, aided by a significant development in military technology.

In 1543 the first Europeans ever to set foot in Japan landed on a small island off the southern coast of Kyushu. They were a group of Portuguese sailors with weapons, including muskets. These weapons made a great impression on Japan's feudal lords, who by this time were called *daimyo.** They were eager to equip their forces with European firearms, and Portuguese traders were quick to oblige them.

As the nature of warfare changed in Japan, it became necessary to build massive castles to resist sieges. Only those daimyo who had the resources to build such castles were able to survive. Three great daimyo in time subdued the others, and by 1600 unity and peace were restored to Japan.

The first of Japan's three "unifiers" was Oda Nobunaga,* a ruthless military chieftain who seized control of Kyoto in 1568 and overthrew the shogunate five years later. In extending his power over central Japan, Nobunaga showed exceptional cruelty. When, for example, the great Buddhist monastery on Mount Hiei* allied itself with Nobunaga's enemies, he destroyed it completely. In the process, his men slaughtered 3,000 people, including villagers who had sought refuge there. Not even children were spared.

Before Nobunaga could conquer all of Japan, he was assassinated by one of his generals. His death was avenged by another of his generals, Hideyoshi.* The second of Japan's unifiers, Hideyoshi was probably the greatest military commander in the nation's history. In

68

Above: a 16th-century picture scroll depicting Portuguese traders in Japan. Below: a preliminary ink and color sketch for a portrait of Hideyoshi.

eight years he marched from one end of the country to another imposing his rule on the daimyo. By 1590 no one dared oppose him further, and Hideyoshi's control of the nation was complete.

Unfortunately, Hideyoshi was carried away by an ambition to conquer China. His armies twice tried to invade China by way of the Korean peninsula, and both times became hopelessly bogged down. When Hideyoshi died in 1598, the samurai abandoned the venture. These were the first — and only — attempts at foreign conquests by Japan's warrior class until modern times.

Hideyoshi died without leaving an adult heir, and a scramble for power among Japan's daimyo followed. The victor in a great battle fought in 1600 was Hideyoshi's foremost vassal, Tokugawa Ieyasu.* He assumed the old title of shogun, and made the town of Edo* — the future Tokyo — his military capital.

Peace and stability. Under Ieyasu and his successors, Japan began a period of peace and stability that lasted for 250 years, a record unmatched by any other country in history. It was accomplished by imposing a series of rigid controls designed to preserve Japan's political and social order as it existed around 1600. Though some changes could not be prevented, these measures assured that much of Japan's feudal system would survive until the second half of the 19th century. The controls imposed by Ieyasu and his successors, known as the Tokugawa shoguns, were as follows:

1. *The daimyo checked.* To keep Japan's daimyo in line, the Tokugawa shoguns developed an effective hostage system. Most of the daimyo were required to spend every other year in Edo to render service at the shoguns' court. The wives and children of the daimyo were required to live in Edo permanently as hostages. This system virtually assured that there would be no daimyo rebellions against the shogunate. To make it foolproof, a

close watch was kept on the roads around Edo to prevent daimyo wives from leaving the city or weapons from being smuggled into it. The system had one other advantage for the shoguns. Each daimyo had to maintain one or more residences in Edo for his family and retainers. This enriched the shoguns' capital city, but it created a serious drain on the finances of the daimyo.

2. *The class structure frozen.* To maintain social stability, the Tokugawa shoguns froze the class structure of Japanese society. Membership in the classes was to be hereditary. Each class was ranked according to its value to society.

The top class was the samurai. Ironically, because of the peaceful conditions that now prevailed in Japan, the samurai's usefulness as warriors was practically at an end. While they still enjoyed the privilege of wearing swords and practiced the arts of war, the samurai now became government administrators, scholars, and teachers. They were strongly imbued with the Chinese philosophy of Confucianism,* which stressed the importance of rule by men of superior education and morality.

Ranking below the samurai were the peasant masses who produced the nation's food. Their only "privileges," however, were to work hard, live frugally, and pay taxes. They were expected to remain on the soil permanently.

Artisans, or craftsmen, ranked below peasants on the social scale. The reasoning that assigned them to an inferior status was that they were not primary producers — the raw materials that they used in their work were produced by others.

Lowest on the social scale were Japan's merchants. Although some of them were quite wealthy, they were held in contempt because they produced nothing themselves, but merely bought and sold. Both merchants and artisans were confined to special quarters within the towns and their activities were closely regulated.

These class divisions reflected the influence of the Chinese philosophy of Confucianism, which the Tokugawa shogunate strongly supported. Confucianism emphasized the need for a harmonious society. In such a society, everyone had a proper "place." Everyone also had duties and responsibilities. If everyone accepted his or her place and duties, there would be peace and order within the society. If not, there would be suffering and chaos. This philosophy was ideally suited to the goals of the Tokugawa shoguns.

3. Japan isolated. The most drastic measures taken by the Tokugawa shoguns to achieve stability were those that isolated Japan from the rest of the world almost completely for more than two centuries.

Since the first Portuguese sailors landed in Japan in 1543, a lively trade had developed with Portugal, Spain, Holland, and England among the European nations. The Portuguese introduced more than firearms to Japan. In 1549 the celebrated Jesuit missionary, Francis Xavier, arrived in Japan seeking converts to the Christian faith. Xavier was impressed with the Japanese. He wrote: ". . . it seems to me that we shall never find among the heathens another race to equal the Japanese. . . . they are men of honor to a marvel, and prize honor above all else in the world." Apparently many Japanese were impressed with Xavier and his successors. By the early 17th century, there were approximately 300,000 Christian converts in Japan, a much higher proportion of the population than is Christian today.

Japan's rulers were friendly to the new religion at first, but gradually they came to see it as a threat to the unity and safety of the country. Japanese Christians, they feared, might owe a higher loyalty to the Pope. And in

At left: Jesuit (left) and Franciscan (right) missionaries walk with two Japanese Christian converts, a young boy and an old man.

many parts of the world, Portuguese and Spanish armies had followed in the wake of missionary activity.

First Hideyoshi and then the Tokugawa shoguns began to persecute Christians. A common practice after 1617 was to order suspected Christians to step on religious images. Those who refused were killed. The final blow against Christianity took place in 1638. At that time, about 37,000 Christian rebels who had been under siege in an old castle near Nagasaki* were slaughtered by the armed forces of the shogun. Christianity as an organized religion was completely crushed in Japan.

The Tokugawa shoguns became increasingly suspicious of *all* foreign influences. European traders were expelled, and Japanese ports were closed to their ships. By 1641 only a limited number of Dutch and Chinese traders were allowed to do business in Japan. They were restricted to a small island in the harbor of Nagasaki and closely guarded.

The Tokugawas were equally harsh toward their own people who were engaged in overseas trade. In 1636 the government forbade all Japanese to go abroad. Japanese residents in foreign countries were forbidden to return. (It was feared that they might have become Christians.) Thousands of Japanese were permanently cut off from their homeland.

Two years later the shogunate banned the construction of ships large enough for overseas trade. Only small ships suitable for trade in Japan's coastal waters were permitted. By such means, the nation was effectively cut off from the rest of the world.

The strict controls imposed by the Tokugawa government had long-lasting effects on the Japanese people. They became accustomed to distinctions of rank, to rules of conduct and etiquette, and to following orders. Obedience and conformity were the price paid for an orderly, stable society.

Cities and merchants. Despite the stern measures taken by the shoguns to preserve Japan's feudal system, it was impossible to prevent change. Peace and unity led to a great increase in internal commerce, and this in turn led to the rapid expansion of towns and cities where merchants did business. By the late 17th century, Japan's urban middle class was beginning to dominate the economic life of the country, and some merchant families became extremely wealthy. At the same time, many samurai were falling on hard times and had to borrow heavily from businessmen. It was not unusual for an impoverished samurai to solve his problems by marrying the daughter of a rich merchant, even though she was at the bottom of the social scale in Tokugawa times.

Merchants display their wares to potential customers in the busy city of Edo, now Tokyo.

The popular arts. As the fortunes of the urban merchants rose, Japan's arts began to reflect their way of life. Puppet plays, called *bunraku,** became quite popular. So did *kabuki,** a new dramatic form that featured elaborate, realistic sets and action that was often violent.

A favorite theme of plays, novels, and short stories was the conflict between duty and love. Typically, a young salesman who is engaged to his boss's daughter falls in love with a beautiful *geisha**—a professional entertainer. Because there is no honorable way that he can break his engagement, his attachment to the geisha is doomed. Finally he and the geisha take the only way out for them—they agree to commit double suicide.

Japanese artists were inspired by the city amusement quarters. They began to paint pictures of the famous actors and geisha who lived and worked there. The development of woodblock printing made it possible to reproduce many copies of a picture and sell them at prices that most city people could afford. In time the artists also

Below: print of 17th-century Kabuki show. Right: Kabuki actors prepare for modern-day performance. Men have played all roles since 1629.

began to paint familiar nature scenes, such as Fuji-yama,* Japan's highest mountain peak. Their woodblock prints were the world's first true mass art and one of the forerunners of the modern picture postcard.

The most popular form of poetry in Tokugawa times was *haiku*,* which reduced the classical short poem from 31 syllables to a mere 17. Despite this severe limitation, some haiku poets were able to convey scenes and moods with great sensitivity. The following poems were written by a noted haiku master, Basho*:

> *An ancient pond*
> *A frog jumps in*
> *The sound of water.*

> *The summer grasses—*
> *Of brave soldiers' dreams*
> *The aftermath.*

Futher signs of change. Increasing trade and expanding cities were not the only signs of change in Japan. Others include the following:

• In 1720 the shogunate lifted its ban on the importation of books from Europe, except those dealing with Christianity. Japanese scholars, who were starved for information about advances in European science and technology, learned the Dutch language from the handful of traders at Nagasaki. Then they avidly studied Dutch books on medicine, astronomy, shipbuilding, gunnery, and other subjects. Eventually they translated them into Japanese. "Dutch learning," as these studies were called, became a valuable asset to Japan when the nation finally embarked on a course of modernization in 1868.

• Education and literacy expanded greatly during Tokugawa times among the samurai, the merchant class, and even the more prosperous peasants. By 1850 about 45 percent of the male population and 15 percent of the female population could read and write. These rates compared well with those of many European nations.

• Ethnic pride became a major force in Japanese life. Two centuries of isolation created a strong sense of distinctiveness among the Japanese and a pride in native traditions. Historians and Shinto priests found in Japan's ancient myths the unique virtues that made their nation "superior." They emphasized the divine ancestry of its emperors and helped to revive respect for the imperial family at Kyoto. Some Japanese even began to wonder why they were ruled by a shogun instead of the emperor.

Encounter with the West. In many ways Japan had outgrown its old feudal structure and was ready for a more modern political and social system. Yet the Tokugawa shogunate still held a firm grip on the country in the first half of the 19th century. It would take an outside force to bring down the old feudal order. This force appeared in Edo Bay (now Tokyo Bay) on July 14, 1853, in the form of a powerful U.S. Navy squadron commanded by Commodore Matthew Perry. The squadron, which consisted of two steamships and two sailships, astonished the Japanese. They had never seen steamships before, nor had they ever seen such huge cannons. It was obvious to them that their own cannons were no match for the firepower of the American warships.

What was the purpose of Perry's visit? For some time American whaling ships had been operating in the waters around Japan. American clipper ships bound for China also passed close to the islands. The United States government had requested permission for these ships to enter Japanese ports to take on supplies, but it had been refused. Other nations had made the same request and were also turned down. Finally, in 1853, U.S. President Millard Fillmore sent Commodore Perry to Japan with a letter demanding that Japan open its ports to U.S. ships and trade.

The opening of Japan. The great majority of Japanese were strongly against allowing foreigners into their country. But the shogun's government knew that it was hopeless to try to resist the guns of the U.S. Navy squadron. It signed a treaty with the United States in 1854 that opened two Japanese ports to U.S. ships to take on supplies. Four years later Japan signed a commercial treaty with the United States permitting full trade in several of its ports.

The right of the Japanese government to impose tariffs was sharply limited. This treaty also granted "extraterritoriality" to Americans in Japan. This meant that Americans accused of breaking the law had the right to be tried by their own consular courts. European powers soon made similar treaties with Japan. The door was now wide open to foreign merchants and residents.

The end of the shoguns. These "unequal treaties" angered the Japanese. In the provinces, many samurai leaders wanted to oust the foreigners by force. Occasionally young samurai would assassinate Western diplomats and traders, or shogunate officials associated with the policy of surrender. More and more, the provincial samurai began to look toward the emperor as an alternative to the discredited government of the shogun. The shogunate had failed to defend Japan against the foreigners and was considered incapable of organizing resistance to them. The slogan of the militant samurai became, "Honor the emperor and expel the barbarians!"

In 1863 samurai forces in Japan's western provinces rose against the Edo government. Within five years they toppled the shogunate and announced, on January 3, 1868, the "restoration" of rule by the emperor. Japan was about to enter a turbulent new age in which it would undergo rapid and far-reaching changes.

Top left: depiction of signing of first commercial treaty between U.S. and Japan. Bottom: Japanese statesman is honored.

Double-check

Review

1. What does *shogun* mean in English? Who was the first Japanese ruler to take this title?

2. What was the system of feudalism based on and how long did it last in Japan?

3. List six values emphasized in the samurai code.

4. List four art forms which were strongly influenced by Zen monks and which still flourish in Japan. What three things do the art forms emphasize?

5. How long was Japan isolated from the rest of the world by the Tokugawa shoguns?

Discussion

1. What is your reaction to the samurai code? Were its ideals noble, realistic, bizarre? Would you have wanted to be a samurai? Why, or why not?

2. How did the contributions of Zen Buddhism to Japanese society alter the Japanese culture previously "borrowed" from China from the sixth to the ninth centuries? What changes did Confucianism bring?

3. Despite the stern measures of the Tokugawa shoguns to prevent it, change came to Japanese society. In fact, it might be said that some of the stern measures taken to prevent changes actually caused changes. Which measures seemed to work this way? Is change inevitable in all societies? Explain your answers.

Activities

1. Some students might research and report to the rest of the class on the similarities and differences between feudalism in Japan and feudalism in Europe during the Middle Ages. Afterward two students might role-play a conversation between a Japanese samurai and a European knight.

2. Eight groups of students might work together to familiarize themselves with one of the following Japanese arts and then give oral reports and demonstrations to the rest of the class: tea ceremony; landscape gardening; flower arrangement; landscape painting in ink; bunraku; kabuki; haiku poetry; tanka poetry.

3. Some students might pretend to be the last Tokugawa shogun, writing his last entry in his diary in which he tries to justify to himself the harsh measures he took to prevent change in Japanese society and what he thinks will happen to Japan when he dies.

Skills

USING AN INDEX

Use the listings above from an index to another book and information in Chapter 4 to answer the following questions.

1. In what order are topics listed in an index?

2. What do the numbers after each topic stand for?

3. On how many pages are Chinese inventions discussed?

4. On what page does the last mention of war with Japan appear?

Read over the first two pages of Chapter 4 and write, on a separate sheet of paper, the following words that appear there: bushido, Kyoto, Yoritoma, samurai, Kamakura. *Then prepare an index for the first five pages of the chapter, using only these words but noting all references to them in the proper form.*

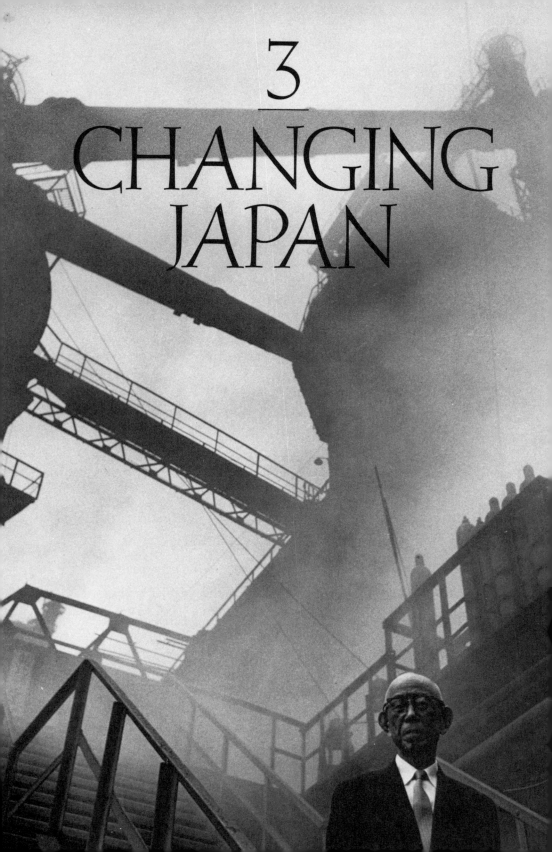

3
CHANGING
JAPAN

Chapter 5

Beginning of Modernization

NOW THAT THE SHOGUNATE had been overthrown, who was going to rule Japan? The militant young samurai who led the rebellion against the Tokugawa government had promised to restore rule by the emperor. In 1868, however, Japan's emperor, Mutsuhito,* was a 15-year-old boy. Even if he had been an adult, there was little chance of his exercising real power. While the samurai leaders were deeply devoted to the emperor, basically they believed that they should make the decisions of government for him. The emperor would remain a symbol of the nation rather than wield real power. In 1869 the emperor was moved from Kyoto to the shogun's castle in Edo, which was then renamed Tokyo, which means "Eastern Capital."

The period of the emperor's reign, from 1868 to 1912, was called *Meiji,** which means "Enlightened Rule." The early part of his reign is known in Japanese history as the Meiji Restoration.

Young Emperor Mutsuhito and his entourage entering Tokyo Castle, the new imperial residence.

The need to modernize. Japan's new leaders had promised — or, at least, threatened — to oust all foreign intruders. They were much too realistic, however, to attempt to "expel the barbarians" by force. In 1863, for example, Japanese coastal forts in the province of Choshu* fired on a number of foreign merchant ships. Soon after, a fleet composed mainly of British warships bombarded the forts and completely destroyed them.

The lesson was clear to Japan's new leaders. If their country was to be able to defend itself against the nations of the West, it must modernize. This meant making Japan a first-rate industrial and military power. The new slogan of Japan's samurai leaders became: "Enrich the country and strengthen its arms."

Before Japan could modernize, however, it first had to end the feudal system that had held back change for so long. Within a few years Japanese society was transformed by a series of revolutionary measures carried out by the new government. Ironically, the political leaders who uprooted the old order were almost all members of the samurai class that had dominated Tokugawa society. Among the most important steps they took to end the feudal system were the following:

1. Japan's feudal lords, or daimyo, were persuaded to give up their domains and their authority. The nation was then divided into new political units, called prefectures, that were directly controlled by the Tokyo government. The daimyo, who received generous payments from the government for their losses, soon faded into obscurity.

2. The samurai were deprived of all their hereditary privileges as a warrior class, including the right to wear swords. Universal military service was adopted to meet the needs of Japan's armed forces.

3. All class divisions and restrictions were abolished, and legal equality was decreed for all Japanese.

The samurai comprised about six percent of the population. Although they received some payment for the loss of their privileges, many were deeply resentful and sometimes rebelled. Finally, in 1877, about 40,000 of them revolted against the Tokyo government. After bloody fighting, the rebellion was crushed by the new drafted army, which was composed mainly of peasants.

What happened to Japan's samurai? A few of them, as

we have seen, now dominated the government. Many became officers in the new army and navy. Others became leaders in business and education. But most were unable to cope with the new conditions. They became poor workingmen, indistinguishable from any others.

Borrowing from Western culture. As Japan's leaders removed feudal barriers to change, they pushed the nation into a rapid program of modernization. The men who had seized power in 1868 to "expel the barbarians" now told the Japanese people that they must emulate the "civilization and enlightenment" of the Western nations. Quite soon railroads, steamships, telegraph lines, and textile mills began to appear in Japan, especially around Tokyo and Yokohama. The government itself developed a number of industries, including armaments and mining. It also pioneered in the building of a variety of factories. Later when the government needed money, it sold many of these enterprises to private businessmen.

To carry out its program of modernization, the government needed to acquire the advanced skills of the Western nations. Select groups of young men were sent abroad to study medicine, law, engineering, business methods, and military technology, among others. Many foreigners were hired at great expense to come to Japan as teachers and advisers. For two decades the Japanese borrowed from Western culture on a much greater scale than they had ever before borrowed from China.

A modern industrial society required a work force that had at least a basic education, plus a large number of highly trained technicians and managers. In 1871 the government began to build thousands of schools from elementary through university level. A six-year elementary school education was made compulsory for all Japanese children. By about 1900 Japan's literacy rate rose to over 90 percent. This was the highest in Asia, and higher than in most other countries of the world.

*Above: Japan's first spinning mill to use
mass-production methods opened in 1872.
Below: busy Yokohama waterfront in 1870.*

Changes in styles and customs. The craze to "become Western" affected the Japanese people in such everyday matters as how to dress, how to wear their hair, and what to eat. Men in the cities began to wear Western clothes, but often in combination with their native attire. It was not unusual, for example, to see the traditional *kimono** (a loose robe tied with a broad sash) worn with long pants, or *hakama** skirts worn with suit jackets. Women's styles changed more slowly, but by the 1880's city women were beginning to wear dresses instead of kimonos.

Hair — and what to do about it — became a big issue. Before 1868, Westerners were often denounced as "hairy barbarians" because of their abundant beards and mustaches. Western men, however, cut their hair fairly short. But when the emperor himself began to sport a beard and mustache, other prominent Japanese felt obliged to do the same. Japanese men let their hair grow long and then tied it in a topknot. But now the government denounced this custom as primitive and unbecoming. Japan's armed forces were the first to cut off their topknots. They did so because it was the only way they could wear their new Western-style military caps. Eventually all Japanese men followed their lead.

The Japanese people had never been meat-eaters. Their Buddhist faith revered all life and forbade eating animals. The new government, however, called this "nothing but bigotry." It told the people that meat would keep them "in good spirits and strengthen the blood." Freed of the taboo against eating meat, some students created a new dish called *sukiyaki.** A mixture of beef, beans, and other vegetables, it has since become a favorite of many foreigners.

In their enthusiasm for Western ways, some Japanese even suggested that English should become the national language.

This woodblock print, depicting a struggle between traditional Japanese objects and Western novelties, illustrates the Japanese reaction against Western ways in the 1880's.

A reaction against Western ways. Not all Japanese shared the enthusiasm for becoming Western. In the 1880's many of them began to urge the nation to retain its own cultural identity. Modern technology, they said, was useful, but Japanese spiritual and moral values were superior to those of the West. The belief that Japan had strayed too far from its traditions of loyalty, duty, and obedience apparently was shared by the Meiji government. Since 1872, Japanese schools had encouraged children to think for themselves. In the 1880's the government announced a change. From now on, it said, the object of education would be to teach children:

- reverence for the emperor;
- loyalty to the nation and state;
- respect for their parents, elders, and teachers.

The new policy meant that children would be taught *what* to think, rather than *how* to think. Japan's elementary schools soon became a powerful instrument for indoctrinating the young with the ideas of the government, and for encouraging obedience and conformity.

The demand for representative government. Japan's leaders had vigorously championed many Western ways, but they did not believe that their people were ready yet for Western-style democracy. They controlled the government completely and permitted little opposition to their rule. Freedom of speech, the press, and assembly were severely limited.

But opposition arose from former samurai who resented having no role in the government. In a petition to the emperor, they accused Japan's rulers of monopolizing power. The solution, they said, was "an assembly elected by the people" to widen participation in the government. Many city merchants and prosperous peasants supported these samurai. In time they formed two political parties to press their demands for "freedom and people's rights," and a representative form of government.

Japan's rulers could have ignored these demands, but they chose not to. Instead they promised the country in 1881 that it would have both a constitution and an elective parliament (legislature) in nine years. Why did they do this?

• The nations of the West, which they admired so much, had constitutions. To be truly modern, Japan must have a constitution also.

• They hoped that a constitution would favorably impress the Western nations, and persuade them to end the unequal treaties they had imposed on Japan.

The Meiji constitution. The constitution that the Meiji leaders gave the country in 1889 provided only a very limited form of democracy. It was presented to the people as a gift from the emperor, who was described as "sacred and inviolable," and the source of all authority. In reality, however, power remained in the hands of the same group of men who had been ruling Japan since 1868. They continued to make the decisions of government for the emperor, and they chose prime ministers and members of the cabinet from among themselves.

The constitution also provided for a Diet (legislature) composed of two houses. The House of Representatives would be elected by male voters who paid more than 15 yen* (Japanese money) a year in taxes. As a result, only about one percent of the population could vote. The House of Peers would be made up of members of a newly created noble class appointed by the government. The House of Representatives could be held in check by the House of Peers, which had equal authority.

The rights and liberties of the Japanese people were listed in detail, but all of them were qualified by the phrase "within the limits of the law." In other words, liberties could be revoked at any time by government decree.

Critics of the new constitution called it a defeat for democracy. They said it was designed to preserve the power of the men who already ruled Japan. These men were now known as the *genro,** or "elder statesmen." Defenders of the constitution said that the Japanese people did not have enough experience yet with the democratic process to rule themselves.

Although democracy was quite limited, the new constitution proved flexible enough to permit the growth of more popular rule in the future. Perhaps its chief limitation in this regard was that it preserved the myth of a "sacred" emperor as the source of all authority in Japan. This enabled high government officials, who in theory were appointed by the emperor, to claim that they were responsible only to him for their actions. In reality they appointed themselves, and the emperor was merely a figurehead. There were few checks on the power of the genro and leaders of the armed forces.

The hopes of Japan's rulers for an end to the unequal treaties were soon realized. The adoption of a constitution, plus a modern civil service system and a new legal

GROWTH OF JAPAN'S EMPIRE 1895 TO 1933

N W E S

RUSSIAN EMPIRE
(U.S.S.R. 1922)

SAKHALIN
(1905)

KURIL ISLANDS (1875)

MANCHURIA
(1931)

OUTER
MONGOLIA

MANCHUKUO
(1932)

INNER
MONGOLIA

JEHOL
(1933)

Mukden

Peking

LIAOTUNG
PENINSULA (1905)

KOREA
(1910)

Port
Arthur

Seoul

Tsingtao
GERMANY 1898–1914,
JAPAN 1914–1923)

Pusan

JAPANESE
EMPIRE

CHINA

Nanking

Hankow

Shanghai

Yangtze River

Yellow River

RYUKYU ISLANDS (1874)

OKINAWA

Canton

HONG KONG
(BRITAIN)

TAIWAN
(1895)

PHILIPPINE
ISLANDS

	1895
	Treaty of 1905
	1910
	Manchuria 1931, "Manchukuo" 1932
	To Manchukuo, 1933

code modeled after those of the West, seemed to qualify Japan as an "enlightened" country. In 1899 the nations of the West gave up the special privileges they had won from Japan by the threat of force.

Japan acquires an empire. As students of Western civilization, Japan's leaders observed that nations like Great Britain, France, and others used their military and naval might to carve out empires in Asia and Africa. Now that the armed forces of Japan had also become strong, it seemed only logical to the government that Japan too should acquire an empire.

Japan soon fought two wars for control of foreign territories and was successful in both. The first of these wars was with China in 1894–1895. Japan surprised the world by easily defeating its huge, but feeble, neighbor. It annexed the Chinese island of Taiwan and received the same commercial privileges in China that Western nations had already forced from that country.

Japan also sought to control the kingdom of Korea and the Chinese province of Manchuria. Its chief rival for domination of those areas was Russia. In 1904, units of the Japanese navy attacked and crippled a Russian fleet based at Port Arthur, Manchuria. After the attack Japan declared war on Russia and won a series of spectacular victories both on land and sea.

In 1905 U.S. President Theodore Roosevelt acted as mediator between Japan and Russia in peace talks held near Portsmouth, New Hampshire. Russia recognized Japan's supremacy in Korea and gave to Japan its interests in Manchuria. It also ceded to Japan the southern half of the large island of Sakhalin* (see map).

A major world power. Japan's astonishing victory over Russia established it as a major world power. In World War I (1914–1918) Japan extended its power by siding with Great Britain and its allies against Germany. With a minimum of effort Japan acquired Germany's island empire — the Marshall and Caroline Islands, and all the Marianas except Guam, which was a U.S. possession — in the Pacific. At the peace conference held in Versailles, France, Japan sat as an equal partner with the victorious Western allies. Within 50 years Japan had achieved the goals set by the leaders of the Meiji Restoration in 1868 — military security from the West and acceptance as a world power.

Change and strain. Japan had become a world power by transforming itself from a feudal society into a modern industrial nation within a few decades. By contrast, the nations of Western Europe had made the same change gradually over a period of several centuries.

Rapid change had unsettling effects on Japanese society. In the 1920's many people were distressed by the apparent clash between native traditions and modern values associated with the West. Let us see how modernization produced strains and conflicts in Japanese society:

1. The growth of big business. In its haste to industrialize, the Japanese government encouraged the formation of huge business companies known as *zaibatsu,** or "financial cliques." These companies combined a wide variety of enterprises — banking, shipping, trading, mining, manufacturing, and others. Companies like the Mitsui* and the Mitsubishi* were each controlled by a single family. Many Japanese resented the concentration of great wealth in the hands of a small group of zaibatsu families. They felt that these business magnates had too much influence, power, and prestige in Japan.

2. Population growth. During the 17th century Japan's population reached 30 million and then remained at that level until the end of Tokugawa times — 1868. After 1868 there was a dramatic increase, largely because of modern medicine. By 1925 the population had doubled to 60 million and was increasing at the rate of one million a year.

Despite Japan's industrial growth, the number of jobs could not keep pace with the number of people. In rural areas, where half the people lived, "surplus" young men migrated to the cities in search of work. Often they found that there was none, or that wages were very low. They became a great reservoir of "cheap labor."

Many people who remained on the farms were no better off. By 1920 almost half of Japan's peasants were reduced by poverty to the status of tenants. They worked on land owned by others and paid the rent with a share of the food they produced.

During the 1920's tenant farmers and urban workers aggressively demanded improved conditions. In rural Japan, disputes between tenant-farmer organizations and landlords flared up. In the cities workers joined trade unions, went on strike, and held mass rallies. By 1929 the number of union members in industry reached 300,000.

3. The growth of cities and mass culture. Japan's cities began to look more and more like those of Western Europe and the United States. This was especially true after 1923, when an earthquake and fire destroyed half of Tokyo. To prevent another such disaster, the city was rebuilt with many steel and concrete structures. Wide avenues replaced once-narrow streets in the downtown area. Soon other cities began to emulate Tokyo with modern office buildings, schools, movie houses, stadiums, and railroad stations. By this time Tokyo had more than two million people, and Osaka had well over one million.

As Western architecture made its appearance in Japanese cities, so did the mass culture of the West. During the 1920's many young girls in the United States began to wear short dresses and skirts, and also cut their hair short. They were called "flappers." Many city girls in Japan copied these styles. They were called *moga*,* short for the English words "modern girl." Their boyfriends

This 1923 Tokyo street scene shows men wearing Japanese kimonos and Western-style hats.

were known as *mobo,** short for "modern boy." American movies, jazz, and styles of dancing became quite popular, especially among the young. There were other signs of American mass culture — musical shows with chorus girls, dance halls, and bars. America's national pastime, baseball, became Japan's national sport too. Babe Ruth, America's greatest baseball hero of the time, was also idolized by Japanese fans. Other Western sports, like tennis, track and field, and swimming, became almost as popular as baseball.

Western social customs also made some headway among young people in the cities. Traditionally, Japanese parents acted as matchmakers for their children and arranged marriages for them. Parents believed that young people were too impractical to choose suitable marriage partners themselves. Now, however, some young people insisted on making their own choices, guided solely by love. Traditionally too, Japanese girls were taught to become obedient, hardworking housewives. That was a duty they owed their husbands. But now many girls worked in offices and some were beginning to question whether women should be little more than household servants.

The Western life-style that was developing in the cities bewildered and offended many Japanese. Older people were shocked by the behavior of the "modern" girls and boys. In the rural areas, which were hardly touched by Western influences, most people still believed in the old values — family solidarity, obedience to authority, duties, and obligations. Distrust and disapproval of city ways were common. This attitude was shared by most of Japan's army and navy officers. They believed that the cities were corrupting the young and making them "soft." The cities were a threat to Japan's warrior traditions of toughness, self-discipline, and loyalty to superiors. Among these groups and others there was a longing for the past, for a return to a simpler, more harmonious, and more authoritarian Japan.

4. The growth of democracy. The men who gave Japan a constitution in 1889 — the genro — believed that they could continue to rule with little interference from the Diet. But the politicians elected to the House of Representatives were not easily put down. Soon organized into political parties, they used their power over the budget to gain important concessions from the Meiji rulers. If the genro wanted more money for the government, they would have to share power. This meant that party leaders would have to be included in the cabinet. In time party leaders were chosen as prime ministers.

By the 1920's Japan developed a democratic system of government that outwardly was similar to Great Britain's. The country was governed by a prime minister and a cabinet chosen from the majority party in the House of Representatives. At the same time, tax qualifications for voting were gradually lowered, permitting more people to take part in elections. In 1925 tax qualifications were removed completely. All Japanese men now had the right to vote.

Democracy in Japan seemed to be secure, but in reality it was threatened by a number of weaknesses. Under the Meiji constitution, powerful officials, including the leaders of the armed forces, could claim that they acted for the emperor and were responsible only to him. They were above control by elected party politicians. Beyond this, most Japanese had no deep commitment to democracy. Many of them, in fact, distrusted it. There was a widespread belief that Japan's major political parties were corrupt and were controlled by the zaibatsu business combines.

The politicians themselves seemed to distrust democracy. In 1925, the same year that all Japanese men acquired the right to vote, the Diet passed a law that made it a crime to advocate a basic change in the political system or the abolition of private property. The Peace Preservation Law, as it was called, was one of a series of repressive laws dating back to Meiji times that gave the police considerable control over freedom of speech and assembly. Although the new Peace Preservation Law was aimed primarily at radical and leftist groups, it could apply to almost anyone who criticized the government.

Depression and crisis. The weakness of the democratic system became apparent in the early 1930's when a worldwide depression crippled Japan's trade. As the nation's foreign markets shrank, hard times set in. Extreme nationalist groups believed that the solution to the problem was to expand Japan's empire by military conquest. Both the government and the zaibatsu, however, were opposed to military conquest. They believed that Japan's economic security depended on peaceful trade and international cooperation.

In the early 1920's the government had signed a treaty with the United States and Great Britain that was designed to limit the size of their navies. Japan agreed to have fewer battleships and aircraft carriers than the Western powers in return for their promise not to build any bases between Hawaii and Singapore. The Japanese government also cut its military budgets at home by more than half and reduced the size of its army.

Leaders of the armed forces were angered by these policies. They believed that the nation's proud military traditions were being betrayed. They had many supporters among the peasants, who made up the bulk of army and navy conscripts. For most peasants service in the armed forces was an exciting alternative to the drudgery of working in the rice fields. In school they had been taught reverence for the emperor and the nation, and the "glory" of dying for them in combat. Many of these conscripts were thrilled that they could now follow in the footsteps of the samurai nobility of old.

Japanese nationalism was also fanned by long-standing opposition in the United States, Canada, and Australia to Oriental immigration. In 1908 the United States and Japan worked out a Gentlemen's Agreement that greatly reduced Japanese immigration to the U.S. This agreement failed to satisfy some U.S. Western states. Then in 1924 the U.S. Congress passed a new immigration act that barred virtually all Orientals as aliens who were ineligible for citizenship. Many Japanese and other Orientals were deeply resentful.

Militarism takes over. As the worldwide depression deepened, those who favored military conquest as a solution to Japan's problems became bolder. Japan already dominated part of Manchuria, but now its military leaders

*In 1931, Japanese troops marched through
the main gate in the ancient wall around
Mukden, the capital city of Manchuria.*

wanted to take over the province completely. Manchuria was much larger than Japan itself and contained valuable raw materials. In 1931 a group of army officers blew up a section of tracks on the South Manchurian Railway, which Japan owned. The Japanese blamed the "Manchurian incident" on the Chinese, and a Japanese army based in Korea quickly moved in to "restore order." Within a few months the army overran the entire province and established a puppet state called *Manchukuo.**

What was the reaction of Emperor Hirohito (who had come to the throne in 1926) and the civil government leaders? Both were opposed to the army's aggression in Manchuria but were helpless to deal with it. The government, which feared that the armed forces would overthrow it if it tried to halt the Manchurian adventure, yielded.

At home the public was elated by the army's easy conquest of Manchuria, and patriotic feelings ran high. In Geneva, Switzerland, the League of Nations (a peacekeeping organization similar to today's United Nations) condemned Japan's aggression. Japan's answer was to withdraw from the League.

Nationalistic young officers in both the army and the navy now began a campaign of terror against government leaders opposed to military conquest. In 1932 they assassinated Prime Minister Inukai,* who was the last member of the Diet to head a government until after World War II. From then on, army and navy leaders increasingly dominated the cabinet. Even so, some young army officers felt that the government wasn't moving fast enough toward further conquests. In 1936 they led a rebellion in Tokyo to overthrow the government. Several officials, including high-ranking members of the armed forces, were killed before the rebellion was suppressed. The army officially disapproved of such deeds but used them to intimidate opponents of its policies. The Japanese public openly admired the young officers who resorted to terrorism against "corrupt" leaders.

World War II begins. Japanese expansion in north China led to a full-scale war with the Chinese in 1937. Japan's armies won victory after victory, but the Chinese forces retreated inland and continued their resistance. The war in China dragged on, taking a heavy toll on Japan's resources.

At home Japan's military leaders tightened their control over the government and repressed political opposition. Hundreds of left-wing politicians, labor leaders, and university students were thrown in prison and tortured until they renounced their views. In 1940 the government forced all political parties to dissolve.

The outbreak of World War II in Europe in 1939 created new opportunities for Japan's military leaders. They proclaimed their intention of creating a vast empire in Asia. They called their grand design the Greater East Asia Co-Prosperity Sphere.

After German armies crushed France in June 1940 Japan's leaders signed a treaty of alliance with Europe's Fascist partners, Germany and Italy. Japanese troops also began moving into Indochina, which was then a French colony.

Until the summer of 1940 the United States had done little more than make futile diplomatic protests against Japanese aggression. It was selling to Japan large amounts of scrap iron, oil, and other raw materials, all of which were essential to the Japanese war machine. Now, however, the United States Congress authorized President Franklin D. Roosevelt to limit or halt the sale of strategic war materials to Japan. In July 1940 President Roosevelt ordered a halt to the shipment of some materials to Japan. The following year, after Japan took over Indochina completely, President Roosevelt shut off *all* U.S. shipments to Japan, including oil.

JAPANESE CONQUESTS
1931 TO 1945

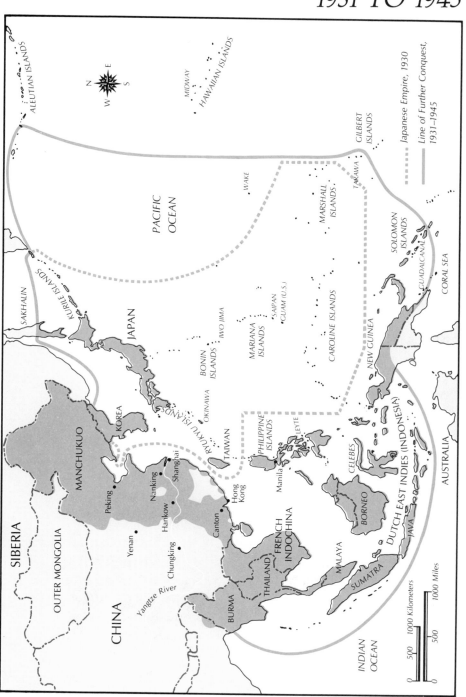

Japanese Empire, 1930

Line of Further Conquest, 1931–1945

ALEUTIAN ISLANDS

MIDWAY

HAWAIIAN ISLANDS

PACIFIC OCEAN

WAKE

GILBERT ISLANDS

TARAWA

MARSHALL ISLANDS

SOLOMON ISLANDS

GUADALCANAL

CORAL SEA

SAKHALIN

KURILE ISLANDS

JAPAN

SAIPAN

GUAM (U.S.)

IWO JIMA

BONIN ISLANDS

MARIANA ISLANDS

CAROLINE ISLANDS

NEW GUINEA

KOREA

OKINAWA

RYUKYU ISLANDS

TAIWAN

PHILIPPINE ISLANDS

LEYTE

CELEBES

MANCHUKUO

Peking

Nanking

Shanghai

Hong Kong

Manila

BORNEO

DUTCH EAST INDIES (INDONESIA)

AUSTRALIA

SIBERIA

OUTER MONGOLIA

Yenan

Harbin

Chungking

Canton

FRENCH INDOCHINA

THAILAND

MALAYA

SUMATRA

JAVA

CHINA

Yangtze River

BURMA

INDIAN OCEAN

500   1000 Kilometers

500   1000 Miles

Without U.S. oil Japan's industry and armed forces would grind to a halt within a year. The leaders of Japan were now faced with a critical dilemma. In order to buy American oil, they were being asked to give up their conquests in China and Indochina. This they were unwilling to do.

The other alternative was to launch a war to seize the Dutch East Indies (Indonesia) where oil was plentiful. Confident that they would be successful, Japan's leaders chose war. It began on December 7, 1941, when Japanese aircraft carriers delivered a devastating surprise attack on the U.S. Pacific fleet at Pearl Harbor, Hawaii. Within a few months Japan's forces overran a vast area of Asia stretching to Australia on the south and India on the west.

Japan is defeated. Eventually, however, the tide of war was turned by the industrial might of the United States. Supplied with a preponderance of warships, planes, and other weapons, U.S. forces gradually advanced toward the Japanese home islands. By November 1944, U.S. warplanes were close enough to Japan to begin bombing and destroying its cities systematically. Two massive fire-bomb raids on Tokyo in the spring of 1945 wiped out most of the city and took more than 100,000 lives.

Though Japan's situation was hopeless, its military leaders refused to surrender. Only after United States warplanes dropped two atomic bombs that virtually wiped out the cities of Hiroshima* and Nagasaki, and killed almost 200,000 people, did the government agree to surrender. The announcement was made by Emperor Hirohito in a broadcast to the Japanese people on August 14, 1945. For the first time in its proud history, Japan had been conquered — and would be occupied — by a foreign nation.

Double-check

Review

1. What role did the samurai leaders in the late 1860's think the emperor should play in the government of Japan?

2. What lesson did Japan's new leaders learn in 1863?

3. What three steps qualified Japan as an "enlightened" country and got Western nations to give up the special privileges they had won from Japan by threat of force?

4. List four changes in Japanese society which produced strains and conflicts during the early 1900's.

5. What resource essential to Japanese industry and armed forces was shut off by the U.S. in 1941?

Discussion

1. You read in an earlier chapter how Japan "borrowed" from Chinese culture, and this chapter discusses the first Japanese craze to "become Western." How do you react to these actions by the Japanese? Most cultures have "borrowed" from others — especially the United States, which was settled primarily by immigrants from other lands. Why do you think this is so? Is such "borrowing" wise or foolish — or neither?

2. In the 1880's the Japanese government outlined specific goals for education. How were these goals similar to the purposes of education in the United States? How were they different?

3. While championing Western ways, Japanese leaders did not believe their people were ready for Western-style democracy. What does it take for a society to be "ready" for democracy? Would the type of education demanded by Japanese leaders in the 1880's prepare people for democracy?

Activities

1. Several students might role-play a conversation in which a young moga and mobo try to explain to their rural and traditional Japanese cousins why they have adopted Western styles.

2. Someone who fought in the United States armed forces against the Japanese in World War II might be invited to speak to the class about his feelings toward the Japanese government and people then and now.

3. An immigrant to the United States from Japan might be invited to speak to the class about her or his experiences in both countries. If possible, try to invite someone who was in the U.S. during World War II.

Skills

Use the two maps in Chapter 5 and information in the text to answer the following questions. On a separate sheet of paper, write the number of each question. Then write the letter (or letters) of the correct answers next to the number of each question.

Answers

A. Southern part of Sakhalin

B. Burma

C. Korea

D. Taiwan

E. French Indochina

F. Guadalcanal

G. Marshall Islands

H. Caroline Islands

1. What territory was acquired by Japan in 1895 after war with China?

2. What territory was acquired by Japan in 1905 under the treaty that ended the war with Russia?

3. What neighboring country did Japan take over in 1910?

4. Name two territories Japan acquired as a result of World War I.

5. What were Japan's farthest conquests to the west and south in World War II?

6. One of the territories above is now split among the countries of Vietnam, Cambodia, and Laos. After Japan seized it in 1941, the U.S. cut off all trade with Japan. Which territory was it?

Chapter 6

Postwar Japan

WHEN U.S. ARMED FORCES began to occupy Japan on September 2, 1945, they found a nation in ruins. Practically all of Japan's cities had suffered great destruction, and their populations were scattered. About two million Japanese had died in the war. More than 600,000 were civilians killed in air raids. Japanese industry was at a standstill, and food production had fallen off one third. Many Japanese wore rags and went hungry. All of them were emotionally numbed. They had followed their leaders blindly, confident that Japanese willpower would carry them to victory. Now they were beaten and exhausted, and foreign soldiers were occupying their country.

Many Japanese feared that the Americans might act cruelly toward them. And many Americans feared that the Japanese, who had fought so fanatically against them during the war, might try to resist the occupation. To the surprise of both sides, the fears proved groundless. The American conquerors generally were fair-minded and friendly. The Japanese were cooperative and even docile. The Americans wanted to reform Japan, and the great majority of Japanese were quite willing to accept their guidance.

Why were the Japanese so open to change? The suffering they endured during the war had turned them bitterly against their former military leaders. The Japanese wanted no more militarism or war. City crowds that had hailed Japanese soldiers as heroes when they went overseas spat on them when they returned home. *Nationalism* and *patriotism* became dirty words, and the Japanese flag was seldom seen. The Japanese people desperately craved peace and a better way of life. The Americans had proved their superiority by defeating Japan in war. Therefore, the Japanese reasoned, democracy must be better than authoritarian rule. They were ready to cooperate with their democratic conquerors.

Japan is demilitarized. The occupation forces in Japan were headed by General Douglas MacArthur, who had been the top U.S. Army commander of the war in the Pacific. He was now designated the Supreme Commander for the Allied Powers, or SCAP, for short. Actually, very few U.S. allies took part in the occupation. Except for some Australian soldiers, it was carried out almost entirely by American forces.

General MacArthur had proven himself a brilliant military leader during the war. Now, however, he was eager to prove himself as a messenger of peace and democracy. His object, he said, was to make Japan "the Switzerland of Asia." Under his direction the following U.S. policies designed to reform Japan were carried out:

• Japan was stripped of all its military conquests, including Taiwan and Korea. More than six million Japanese soldiers and civilians in overseas areas were sent home. The armed forces were completely disbanded, their weapons were destroyed, and all war factories were dismantled.

A tall member of the Military Police draws stares as he walks through the streets of a Japanese city shortly after World War II.

- War criminals, including former government leaders and officers accused of atrocities, were brought to trial.
- All those associated with Japan's policy of military conquest were purged from positions of responsibility in Japanese society. About 200,000 former officers, government leaders, businessmen, and teachers were affected.
- Extreme nationalistic and militaristic organizations were banned.
- Repressive laws were abolished, and all political prisoners were freed.

A new constitution. Most of these reforms were intended to demilitarize Japan. To prevent a return to militarism, however, the United States believed that Japan needed a democratic constitution. When Japanese leaders failed to produce a document that was satisfactory to General MacArthur, he had his own staff write a constitution for Japan. The new constitution, which went into effect on May 3, 1947, was enthusiastically accepted by a great majority of the Japanese people. It specified that:

1. The emperor was merely "the symbol of the state and the unity of the people" and had no political powers at all. (Emperor Hirohito prepared the Japanese people for this change by telling them in a radio broadcast that he was in no sense "divine.")

2. The House of Representatives would have supremacy in the political system. It would elect the prime minister, and both he and his cabinet would be responsible to it. All other power groups were either eliminated or made subordinate to it. The House of Peers, for example, was replaced by an elective House of Councillors with less power than the House of Representatives. By these means parliamentary democracy was made secure.

The constitution also spelled out in detail the rights of the Japanese people. These rights were declared to be "eternal and inviolate." Among them were some that are not included in the U.S. Constitution — equal rights for women, the right of labor to bargain collectively, and the right of everyone to receive an equal education. The vote was extended to all men and women age 20 or older.

Perhaps the most interesting provision of the constitution was its renunciation of war "forever." Japan also renounced the maintenance of "land, sea, and air forces, as well as other war potential." Within a few years this provision would be stretched to allow Japan small Self-Defense Forces.

Economic and social reforms. In their enthusiasm to reform Japan, General MacArthur and his staff went beyond political measures. They believed that democracy in Japan would be stronger if wealth and power were distributed more evenly in the society. To achieve this goal they carried out the following reforms:

• Dozens of zaibatsu companies were disbanded, and the owning families were stripped of most of their wealth. This was called "zaibatsu-busting."

• Graduated income taxes were imposed to make the accumulation of great wealth much more difficult.

• Labor unions were encouraged to expand. Eventually more than 12 million workers joined them.

• Absentee landlords were required to sell all but 2½ acres of their land at a small fraction of its actual value. As a result, tenant farming in Japan was sharply reduced, and the nation's peasants soon became relatively prosperous.

• The nobility and all titles were abolished except for the emperor and his immediate family.

• The legal authority of the head of a family over other adult members was declared invalid.

• Compulsory education was extended from six to nine years. The indoctrination of the young with militaristic and nationalistic propaganda was ended.

These sweeping reforms produced some results that were not expected by the occupation authorities. Japan's labor unions, which were largely connected with the Socialist and Communist parties, seemed less interested in collective bargaining than they were in establishing socialism. There was much political agitation, and huge rallies were held in the streets. The word *demo* became common in Japan, but it stood for demonstration rather than democracy. Yet there was no breakdown of order. Despite the drastic changes produced by the occupation, Japanese society remained disciplined.

A major policy change. In 1948 the emphasis of the occupation changed. U.S. officials became much more concerned with Japan's economic recovery than with reforms, most of which were well under way. Industrial and farm production, however, were still dangerously low, and the Japanese people were living at a bare subsistence level despite U.S. aid. American authorities feared that democracy might not survive in Japan unless the nation's economy was restored.

There was another important reason for the shift in U.S. policy. In 1948 the United States was alarmed by the spread of communism in Eastern Europe and China. Hostility between the United States and the Soviet Union was intensifying. (This period of intense hostility became known as the *Cold War* — a political and economic confrontation that stopped short of actual shooting.) It now appeared to the United States that a democratic, economically strong Japan could be a valuable ally in the struggle to contain the spread of communism.

Reforms that seemed to conflict with economic recovery were either modified or dropped. The further breakup of many large companies was halted. Strikes that might endanger production were restricted.

These changes infuriated Japanese leftists. Increasingly they began to denounce the occupation and its policies. Other Japanese also became critical. Many of them questioned whether everything the Americans did was good, or whether everything distinctively Japanese was bad. Some saw a contradiction between the desire of the United States to democratize Japan and the absolute authority of the occupation force. Others were irritated by the continued presence of foreign soldiers who enjoyed luxuries that few Japanese could afford.

The occupation ends. The honeymoon of the occupation authorities with the Japanese people was clearly over. It was time now, the United States believed, to end the occupation and allow the Japanese to govern themselves. Unfortunately the Soviet Union stood in the way of a formal peace treaty with Japan that would end the occupation. The Soviet Union demanded the right to participate in a peace conference and to veto any of its decisions. Finally the United States decided to go ahead without the Soviet Union. In 1951 a peace treaty was concluded making Japan an independent nation once again. More than 40 countries signed the treaty, but not the Soviet Union or Communist China.

The United States committed itself to defend Japan in case of war. A separate Security Treaty between the two countries provided for keeping American bases in Japan. For the Japanese people the future now looked much more hopeful than had seemed possible in September 1945.

Japan's economic miracle. The widespread misery to which Japan had been reduced in 1945 was slow to disappear. By 1950 the worst poverty had been lessened. But the annual income per person was still only $132, an extremely low level for an industrial nation.

In 1950, however, Japanese industry received an unexpected boost from the outbreak of war in Korea. Following World War II, Korea was divided into two countries — North and South Korea. North Korea, ruled by a Communist government, invaded South Korea in June 1950. The United States and other members of the United Nations quickly dispatched armed forces to prevent a Communist takeover of South Korea. To help supply its forces in Korea, the United States bought large quantities of goods from Japan.

The entire Japanese economy began to pick up and continued to gain momentum even after the Korean war ended in 1953. By the 1960's Japan's gross national product (the total value of production and services) was increasing by 10 percent a year, a rate unequaled by

Wearing a postwar mixture of Japanese and U.S. clothing, these hired musicians try to lure business to a shopping center near Tokyo.

any other nation in the world. Annual income per person rose to well over $1,000. Meanwhile population growth began to decline until it reached a level of only one percent a year. (The chief reason was probably the desire of most parents to give their children as much education as possible. Financially it would be easier to educate two or three children than more.)

Prosperity. With more money to spend than ever before, the Japanese people went on a buying spree. Before long almost every family had a television set and a camera. Small washing machines, refrigerators, and electric rice cookers became standard equipment in homes. Many homes also had air conditioners, and many families even had a car.

Rural Japan shared in the prosperity. New insecticides and chemical fertilizers were used lavishly to increase food production. The introduction of machines like miniature tractors and motorized threshers also helped. By

116

the mid-1950's Japanese farmers were producing crops that far surpassed prewar levels. TV antennas, motorcycles, and small trucks became familiar sights in the countryside. By the 1960's some Japanese farmers were prosperous enough to buy cars or take vacations in Hong Kong, Hawaii, and Europe.

Japan was rapidly regaining and expanding its foreign trade. Before World War II, the label "Made in Japan" was usually associated with cheap, shoddy goods. Now, however, Japan concentrated on developing high-quality products for export. Its textiles, cameras, and electronic equipment soon began to flood the markets of the world. Later came Japanese ships, steel, machinery, cars, and computers. By the end of the 1960's the nation's exports were exceeding its imports considerably. In 1985 its trade surplus amounted to more than 49 billion dollars!

The reasons why. How did Japan achieve its economic miracle? Much of it was due to hard work. The Japanese people had usually extended themselves when natural disasters struck their land. In 1945 they set about with the same determination to restore their bombed-out cities and industrial facilities. Hard work, however, was not the whole story. Japan's recovery was spurred by other factors:

• Japanese labor was highly skilled, yet its wages were relatively low by Western standards. This gave Japanese industry a competitive edge in the world's trade markets.

• Bombed-out factories were replaced by new ones using the latest and most efficient equipment. This also gave Japan an edge over nations whose equipment was often less modern.

• Technical know-how imported mainly from the United States greatly helped to step up Japan's industrial growth. The Japanese government worked closely with industry to assure that only the latest and best developments in technology were acquired.

• Japan was relieved of the burden of supporting large military and naval forces by its constitution and the commitment of the United States to defend it. In 1980 the cost of Japan's small Self-Defense Forces was less than one percent of its gross national product. This compared with seven percent for the United States.

Social problems. Industrial growth brought the Japanese people greater wealth than they had ever enjoyed before, but it also produced new problems or worsened old ones. As more and more people left the farms to find work in urban factories, Japan's cities became perhaps the most overcrowded in the world. Although Tokyo, Osaka, and other cities built impressive high-rise office buildings, much of their housing would be considered slums in the United States. Hospitals, schools, parks, and sewage systems were also neglected in the rush to build steel mills, shipyards, and other industrial facilities. Above all, industrial wastes heavily polluted the nation's air, water, and land. The following story, which appeared in *The New York Times* in March 1973, describes a pollution case that shocked the Japanese public:

"In the fishing town of Minamata* 20 years ago, cats began dancing in the streets and fell dead. . . . Dogs and pigs went mad. Crows dropped from the sky.

"Then the mysterious malady struck human beings. It destroyed their control over their arms and legs, made them blind and deaf, and killed them. It affected babies in their mothers' wombs and condemned them to live after birth as vegetables.

"Last week the storm stirred up by this phenomenon ended in a court decision that underscored the growing concern about pollution in Japan.

"Medical researchers had determined by the late

Holding her dead daughter's photo, a Japanese mother protests her death in the Minamata pollution disaster.

1950's that the victims had been poisoned by mercury. They traced the mercury to fish and shellfish eaten by the victims. The mercury, in turn, was traced to sludge at the bottom of Minamata Bay, dumped by the chemical plant of the Chisso* Corporation.

"The company denied it was responsible, and some of the victims eventually went to court in 1969. The case ended last week when a district judge ruled that Chisso was at fault and ordered it to pay 3.6 million dollars in damages to 138 persons in 30 families. It was the highest industrial pollution claim yet awarded in Japan. The company accepted the decision and agreed to compensate other victims who had not gone to court.

"The Minamata decision was one of four major court tests here. All ended in favor of the victims. Together the decisions set a legal precedent holding industrial companies liable for the effects of their pollution and gave new stimulus to demands that Japan be cleaned up.

"In a recent published survey, Ui Jun, a chemical engineer at Tokyo University and an authority on pollution, says, 'We Japanese are living in the most heavily polluted country in the world.' He blames it on 'the rapid development of the economy . . . and the degenerate use of science and technology.' "

Changes in society. Japan's economic miracle, combined with the occupation reforms, produced many changes in Japanese society. Among them are the following:

• Extremes of wealth and poverty were sharply reduced and are now less marked than in the United States. The war and the occupation reforms wiped out most great fortunes, while postwar affluence raised the standard of living of the masses generally. Japan has no large "underprivileged" minorities and is a largely middle class society.

• Young people deserted rural areas in droves, attracted by the excitement of the cities and factory jobs that were less arduous than farm work. In some rural areas 90 percent of the young moved to cities after completing their education. Many adult male farmers began to commute during the week to factory jobs in nearby cities. More and more, farming in Japan was done by women and elderly parents. Less than 20 percent of the population now works on farms.

• A typical Japanese family shrank to four people — mother, father, and two children. Fewer grandparents or other relatives lived with them under the same roof.

• Young men and women became increasingly independent of the authority of the male head of the family.

Japan's relations with the U.S. The single most controversial political issue in postwar Japan centered on the nation's relations with the United States. Specifically, the issue was whether Japan should continue to ally itself with the United States or become strictly neutral in foreign affairs. Support for the alliance came mainly from the Liberal Democratic Party which has ruled Japan since 1955. Contrary to its name, this is Japan's leading conservative party. Opposition to the alliance came mainly from Japan's left-wing parties, above all the Socialists and the Communists. Yet at times opposition had great popular appeal and was shared in part by many of Japan's conservatives.

Much of the opposition stemmed from the terrible suffering the Japanese endured in World War II. They were now deeply committed to peace. They wished to avoid involvements in international disputes as much as possible. To many Japanese the Security Treaty with the United States seemed potentially dangerous. In the event that the United States went to war, Japan might be drawn in against its will. And the presence of U.S. military bases in Japan might even invite a nuclear attack from one or another of the U.S.'s enemies.

The memory of the atomic bombings of Hiroshima and Nagasaki in World War II made the Japanese particularly sensitive about nuclear weapons. Memorial meetings held at Hiroshima each year on August 6, the anniversary of the bombing of that city, turned into huge protest demonstrations against the United States and the Security Treaty.

In 1954 the United States conducted atomic tests on Bikini* Island in the mid-Pacific. Fallout from the tests showered a Japanese fishing boat, resulting in the death of one crewman. In Japan the incident aroused tremendous public indignation. Similarly, massive demonstrations greeted the arrival of the first nuclear-powered U.S. submarines in Japan.

The Security Treaty crisis. Opposition to the Security Treaty reached its greatest height in 1960. Ironically, that year the treaty was revised to allay some of Japan's worst fears about it. The major revisions were:

1. The U.S. could not bring nuclear weapons into Japan without the approval of the Japanese government.

2. The United States could not use its forces based in Japan for military action abroad without the approval of the Japanese government.

When the revised treaty was submitted to the Diet for approval, it was opposed by the leftist parties, which wanted no treaty at all. Yet the Liberal Democratic Party had a solid majority in the Diet, and it seemed only a matter of time before the treaty would be approved. Prime Minister Kishi,* however, was impatient to have it approved before the scheduled visit of U.S. President Dwight D. Eisenhower in June 1960. In the early morning hours of May 20, when the Socialist opposition was absent, Kishi suddenly called for a vote on the treaty and won its approval.

Top right: protest against storage of U.S. missiles near Yokohama. Bottom: protest against U.S. nuclear submarine visits.

Many Japanese were thoroughly angered by Kishi's tactics, which they considered high-handed and undemocratic. Communists, Socialists, and other radical groups were quick to take advantage of this reaction and organized protest demonstrations. By June hundreds of thousands of protesters were snake-dancing through the streets of Tokyo and other cities every day, shouting anti-American and antitreaty slogans. Although there was little violence many people feared that democracy in Japan was doomed. On June 16 the government had to ask President Eisenhower to cancel his visit. Almost immediately the disturbances subsided. In July Kishi was replaced by another Liberal Democratic leader, Ikeda,* who promised to respect public opinion and opposition views. Japanese democracy had weathered its greatest postwar crisis, and the Security Treaty with the United States remained intact.

The creation of Self-Defense Forces. As Japan became more and more affluent in the 1960's, the influence of left-wing groups began to decline. Issues that once stirred up public indignation no longer seemed so troublesome. One of these issues was the creation by the government of Self-Defense Forces consisting of relatively small army, navy, and air units. These forces originated in 1950 when the Korean war began. At that time U.S. troops in Japan were hastily sent to South Korea to fight the Communist invasion. To replace these troops the Japanese government organized a National Police Reserve of 75,000 men. The reserve was later expanded and reorganized in 1954 as the Self-Defense Forces. They were limited to 250,000 men, and service was entirely voluntary.

The creation of the Self-Defense Forces, which was supported by the United States, outraged most Japanese. They saw it as the beginning of a return to militarism, and a violation of the nation's constitution.

In the 1960's, opposition to the Self-Defense forces gradually waned, and most Japanese now take them for granted. They are concerned instead with limiting the amount that the Japanese government spends on defense. In 1976 the government ruled that they would spend no more than 1 percent of the country's total economic output on the national defense. Recently, the amount has been increased to 1.4 percent—a projected 16.7 billion dollars for 1986.

Major problems resolved. Problems that have caused tensions between Japan and the United States have, as a rule, been successfully resolved. Among them are the following:

1. Relations with Communist China. For many years the United States had no diplomatic or trade relations with Communist China. The U.S. recognized the Chinese Nationalist government on the island of Taiwan, rather than the Communist government that ruled mainland China. Most Japanese wished to establish friendly relations with mainland China and develop trade with it. The Japanese government, however, would not recognize the Communist government as long as the United States was opposed to it. Like the U.S., Japan continued to recognize the Nationalist government on Taiwan.

Then in 1972 U.S. President Richard M. Nixon paid a historic visit to mainland China. His visit established informal diplomatic relations between the Communist government and the United States, and opened up trade between the two countries.

The Japanese government was shocked, at first, that President Nixon had not consulted with it about his decision to visit China. But once President Nixon removed some of the restraints on relations with that country, the Japanese went one step further. In September 1972 Prime Minister Tanaka* visited mainland China and formally recognized the Communist government. Recogni-

125

tion of the government on Taiwan was withdrawn. (The United States followed suit in December 1978, when President Jimmy Carter took the same action.)

2. *The Vietnam war.* During the 1960's, United States military support of South Vietnam in its conflict with the Communist government of North Vietnam alarmed many Japanese. They feared that Japan's alliance with the United States might eventually involve their country in the war too. The Japanese public deplored U.S. air attacks on North Vietnam, which reminded them of the terrible raids they had suffered in World War II.

Organized protests against U.S. participation in the Vietnam war were often violent, particularly among extreme left-wing student groups. In 1968 student protesters almost wrecked the University of Tokyo, forcing it to close for one year. The withdrawal of U.S. forces from Vietnam, which was completed in 1973, eventually eliminated this source of tension in Japanese-American relations.

3. *The problem of Okinawa.** Near the end of World War II, U.S. forces captured the island of Okinawa, which lies south of the main Japanese islands. The people of Okinawa are a branch of the Japanese, and the island itself had been a part of Japan since 1609. When Japan surrendered in 1945 it had to give up Okinawa. The United States continued to occupy the island as a base for its armed forces in the Pacific. The people of Okinawa had always been treated as "inferiors" by the Japanese on the main islands and had resented it. But now the Okinawans resented U.S. military rule even more and began to demand a return to Japan. By the late 1960's many people in Japan began to sympathize with them. Both nationalistic conservatives and anti-American leftists shared the view that rule of Okinawa by a foreign power was intolerable.

The problem was finally resolved in 1969 when the

United States agreed to give Okinawa back to Japan within a few years. In return, the United States was allowed to keep its bases there under the same limitations as other bases in Japan. Okinawa was finally returned to Japan in May 1972.

Shades of the past. Since the end of World War II, Japan has been committed to a policy of peace and international trade. Even those Japanese who have no memory of the war are convinced that peace is essential to their country's well-being. Yet the spirit of militarism that characterized prewar Japan still comes to the surface on occasion. In the 1960's, for example, Mishima Yukio,* a highly respected author, began to urge the Japanese to return to their samurai traditions. He himself organized a private army of 100 men and dedicated it to the defense of the emperor. On November 25, 1970, Mishima and four of his followers broke into the Tokyo headquarters of the Self-Defense Forces. In an impassioned speech Mishima urged the soldiers to revolt against the government. Many of the servicemen laughed at him. At the end Mishima was true to his samurai code. He plunged a dagger into his abdomen and then was beheaded by one of his followers.

Mishima's act both shocked and thrilled the Japanese people. It failed, however, to win more than a few converts to his cause.

Though the great majority of Japanese continue to reject militarism, other traditions associated with it still appeal to them strongly. The Japanese were deeply moved, for example, by the experiences of two World War II soldiers who held out against "the enemy" until the 1970's. Sergeant Yokoi* remained hidden on Guam until January 1972, when he finally surrendered. Lieutenant Onoda* continued to collect "military intelligence" on an island in the Philippines until March 1974. He did not give up until his former commanding officer came in

*Japanese businessmen politely exchanging
name cards in Tokyo railroad station.*

person to call off Onoda's mission. Most Japanese had no use for militarism, but they greatly admired the loyalty and sense of duty displayed by these two men. Both were treated as heroes.

The problems of success. While many Japanese regret the continued "Westernization" of their country, they know that it is impossible to return to the past. Japan has become an industrial and trading giant, perhaps the most successful in the world today. Its economy now supports a population that is far larger, and much more prosperous, than that of prewar Japan.

Ironically, Japan's great success as an industrial nation is also the cause of most of its problems today. We have already seen some of the terrible consequences of industrial pollution in Japan. Abroad, many nations resent Japan's success. Some Asiatic nations in particular see Japan as an economic "animal," selfishly feeding on their natural resources and dumping its manufactures on them. Some have accused Japanese businessmen of driving hard bargains and using deceitful practices. In 1970, for example, Thailand's Minister of Economic Affairs, Bunchana Atthakor,* made the following charge:

"In business matters, the Japanese are concerned only with making money. . . . Take, for example, the manufacture of irrigation pumps and small tractors. The Japanese work very hard to sell these items. But should the machinery break down, they tell the customer that there are no spare parts, and that he has to buy a new machine. Thanks to such practices, Thai farmers haven't got a chance. They can only become poorer and poorer until they die."

Western nations, including the United States, have also charged Japan with unfair trade practices. After World War II, for example, the United States allowed most Japanese goods to enter the U.S. freely, even when they were in direct competition with American products.

129

Japan, however, limited its imports from the United States mainly to raw materials and other items that did not compete with native products. As a result, a great many U.S. manufactures, including cars, were excluded from Japan.

The United States government accepted this inequality at first in an effort to bolster Japan's weak postwar economy. When Japan became prosperous, many American business people protested that there was no longer any reason to permit it such an advantage. Japan has lifted many restrictions on American imports, but the Japanese people largely still prefer to buy domestically-produced goods. The Japanese government is trying to persuade them to buy more foreign imports, but progress is slow.

Oil and inflation. Japanese industry, as we have seen, is heavily dependent upon foreign nations for many vital raw materials. This weakness struck Japan forcefully in 1973. At that time Arab oil-producing nations halted shipments of crude oil to a number of industrial countries, including the United States and Japan. Shipments were resumed in 1974, but at four times the former price.

Japan was particularly vulnerable to the oil cutoff and the price rise. Much of its industry is fueled by oil, almost all of which is imported from Arab nations. Ever since the oil cutoff, the Japanese have feared that their industries could be halted by a lack of energy resources.

Recently that fear has been greatly lessened. Oil prices fell to a record low in 1986. This has been very good for Japan, but not for the the U.S., which is one of the world's primary oil producers. As a result, the Japanese yen has strengthened against the American dollar, causing a further strain in economic relations between Japan and the U.S. Here are some typical prices that Americans paid in Tokyo in 1985 :

a cup of coffee-$2.00

pizza and beer for one person-$10.00

a pound of sirloin steak-$15.00
an orange-$.50
a movie ticket-$7.50

However, the yen's recent strength against the dollar is no indication of an completely healthy economy. Japan borrows more money than other industrial nations while gaining less revenue from taxes. The result is a huge budget deficit, and not enough money for important social-welfare programs.

The outlook for Japan. Japan in the 1980's faces three major problems:

1.The continuing threat to its environment caused by industrial pollution.

2.The pressure brought by other industrial nations to import more of their products.

3.Reducing a mammoth budget deficit that uses up a large part of the country's revenue in interest payments on loans.

These problems strongly suggest that Japan's industrial growth must slow down further in the years ahead. Some people fear that this will lead to a business depression that could produce serious political and social disorders. Others agree that the country's problems are serious but believe that the Japanese will overcome them. They base their optimism on the following reasons:

• The Japanese have perhaps the highest level of education of any people in the world.

• They are as hardworking and energetic as ever.

• They have a very strong sense of cultural unity.

• They are a highly disciplined people who have endured many shocks in the past with a minimum of disorder. If they could overcome the disaster of World War II, they can surmount the problems that lie ahead.

Double-check

Review

1. Why did the Japanese think that democracy was better than authoritarian rule after World War II?

2. Give two reasons why the United States became more concerned in 1948 with Japan's economic recovery than with reforms.

3. In addition to hard work, list two other factors which spurred Japan's postwar economic recovery.

4. List four major social changes in Japanese society that resulted from the economic recovery and the occupation reforms.

5. List three problems faced by Japan as it entered the 1980's.

Discussion

1. To ensure the strength of democracy, General MacArthur and his staff initiated sweeping changes in many aspects of Japanese society. Could — or should — any of those changes have been carried out in the United States immediately after World War II? Give reasons for your answers.

2. The Japanese constitution of 1947 renounced war "forever." Do you think the Japanese Self-Defense Forces are a threat to this provision? Do you think other nations could — or should — renounce war forever? Explain.

3. This chapter lists three major problems facing Japan in the 1980's and four reasons why some people say Japan should be able to solve the problems. Which problem do you think is the most serious for Japan? Why? Which of the four strengths of Japanese society do you think is its greatest strength? Why?

Activities

1. Some students might play the role of Emperor Hirohito and write a speech for the radio broadcast, telling the Japanese people that he is in no sense "divine." Afterward they might read their speeches aloud.

2. Some students might get a copy of the 1947 Japanese constitution and a copy of the U.S. Constitution and then prepare a report to the rest of the class on differences and similarities in the two documents.

3. Two or more students might pretend to be editors of opposing Japanese newspapers in May 1960. One (or more) editors should write a front-page editorial supporting Prime Minister Kishi's tactics to get approval of the Security Treaty with the U.S., while other editors should write editorials condemning his tactics.

Skills

NEWS ITEM:
CHINA AND JAPAN SIGN
PEACE AND FRIENDSHIP TREATY

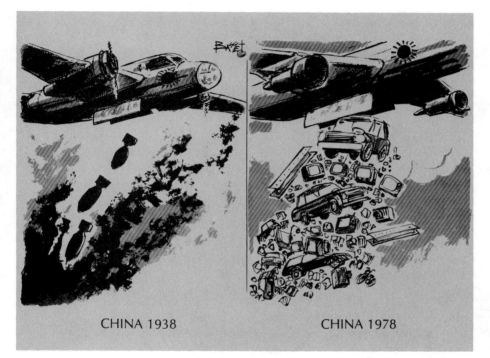

CHINA 1938   CHINA 1978

Use the political cartoon above and information in Chapter 6 to answer the following questions.

1. Whom does the plane on the left represent?
(a) China   (b) Japan   (c) the U.S.

2. On whom is it dropping bombs?
(a) Japan   (b) China   (c) the U.S.

3. What is the plane on the right dropping?
(a) modern bombs   (b) U.S. mail   (c) Japanese manufactures

4. What seems to be the main point of the cartoon?
(a) It's a cloudy day over China.
(b) As a result of the treaty, Japan is "bombing" China with manufactures.
(c) China and Japan are still enemies.

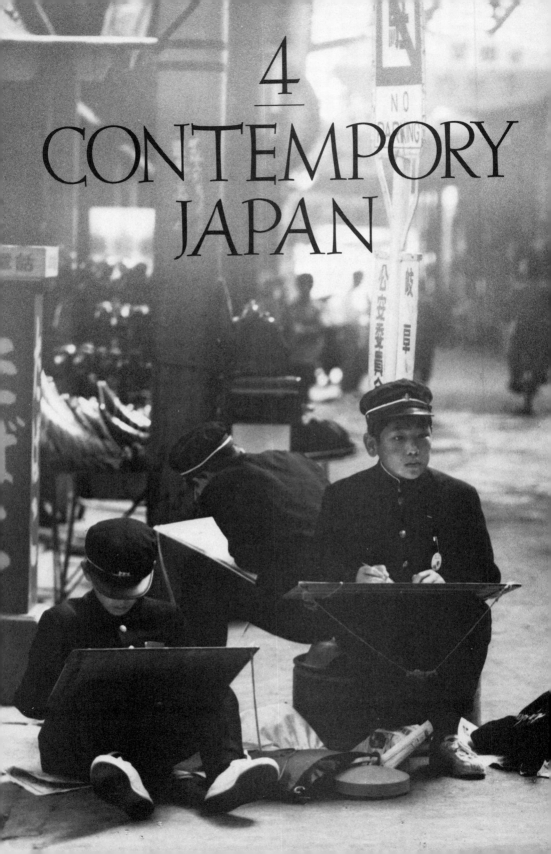

4
CONTEMPORY JAPAN

Chapter 7

Values

WHAT IMAGE DO YOU HAVE of the Japanese people? Do you believe that they are very similar to people of the Western world? Well, in many ways they are. The great majority live in cities complete with high-rise office buildings, traffic-congested streets, neon lights, department stores, and lively amusement quarters. They wear Western-style clothes and travel to work in crowded subways and commuter trains. In their leisure time they enjoy, among other things, television, baseball, bowling, beer, and sight-seeing. Most Japanese housewives take electric appliances for granted, and many of them drive cars. If they have children in school, they are almost certain to belong to the Parent Teacher Association. Japanese children are strongly motivated to do well in school and become successful in their later careers.

A distinctive people. Are the Japanese, then, "just like us"? Modern industrial technology has produced many similarities, but the Japanese remain a very distinctive people with unique traits. Their values and beliefs are likely to be quite different from our own. As a rule, for example, they intensely dislike emotional confrontations. Blunt speech, which may produce hurt feelings or loss of "face" (pride), is carefully avoided. Western businessmen in Japan are often unaware of this and sometimes must be protected from their own tendency to "lay things on the line."

Take the recent case of a Canadian executive in Tokyo who was keenly disappointed in the performance of his Japanese salesmen. He decided that what they needed was a good tongue-lashing, and called them together for that purpose. Speaking in English he said:

"Do you people call yourselves salesmen? You don't know the first thing about selling! It's obvious that you've paid no attention to anything I've told you. I'm surprised that any of you can even look me in the face. Now what do you plan to do about improving your sorry record?"

Fortunately for this executive, his Japanese interpreter was as skilled in diplomacy as he was in languages. This is how he translated the executive's words:

"I have only the highest regard for your selling abilities. However, I would not be completely honest if I did not permit myself to express my disappointment in your recent performance. I trust that you will understand and try to do better in the future."

What would have happened if the interpreter had not toned down the executive's remarks? The result would have been disastrous. The salesmen would have been mortified and would have assumed that the executive was mentally deranged.

Japanese values. To understand how and why the

Japanese differ from us, let's examine some of their beliefs and compare them with our own.

Group loyalty. Perhaps the outstanding characteristic of the Japanese people is their intense loyalty to groups of all kinds. Loyalty means:

• putting the interests of the group above personal interests and ambitions;

• being willing to cooperate with other members and accept the decisions of the group enthusiastically;

• avoiding any situation that might embarrass or shame other members of the group.

In Japan, to bring shame on the group is to dishonor oneself. A daughter, for example, loses the respect of her family and others if she marries without consulting her parents' wishes. Workers lose the respect of their colleagues if they leave the company that employs them to take higher-paying jobs with another company.

Family ties. Before the Meiji Restoration (1868) the most important groups in Japanese society were those of the feudal lord and his samurai retainers, the family, and the rural village. The samurai have long since gone, and village life has declined. But family ties still remain strong in Japan.

As we have seen, however, the Japanese family structure has changed considerably in modern times. Formerly it was customary for three generations of a family — grandparents, children, and grandchildren — to live under the same roof. (Usually the grandparents lived with their oldest son, who inherited the family farm or business.) Today tiny city apartments make such arrangements difficult, if not impossible. Although most elderly parents still live with their children, more and more are beginning to live separately. In such cases they are likely to be in the same neighborhood, sometimes in adjacent houses or apartments.

Formerly too the authority of the male head of the

family over other members was complete. His wife, children, and younger brothers were legally required to obey him. After World War II, his legal authority over other adult members of the family was abolished. One effect was to establish the independence of "branch" families started by younger brothers. Nevertheless many Japanese are still devoted to the older concept of the family and respect its traditions. "Big brother" can no longer dictate to his "little brothers," but his advice and support are likely to be valued by them.

Other than the family, the most important group in Japan today is the company where one works. The relationship between a Japanese company and its employees can be compared to that of the feudal lord and his samurai retainers. The company assures its employees of lifetime security, and in return expects a lifetime of loyal service. Most Japanese employees *are* loyal. They take great pride in their company, especially if it is large and famous. They wear company pins, sing company songs, go on company outings, and participate in company athletic meets. They are good "organization men."

Organized group activities. Most Japanese love group activities and take part in them with enthusiasm. There are organized hobby groups for everything from flower arrangement to judo.* Sight-seeing, to which the Japanese are addicted, is almost always done in groups. These may consist of school classes, work groups, women's societies, youth clubs, and many others. In the society as a whole, life seems to center on groups.

Well, don't Americans belong to groups also? We do, but there is a difference. Even in groups, Americans tend to see themselves as individuals who must be true to their personal ideals. It is important for them to express their originality and independence. The Japanese, however, tend to frown on individualism. In their view it means putting one's own interests ahead of the interests

138

of the group. The Japanese are more likely to admire the team player than the "star," and team spirit more than personal ambition.

Does this mean that the Japanese generally believe in conformity? They would not deny this. One of their favorite proverbs is, "The nail that sticks up gets hammered down." Yet the Japanese do not see conformity as a kind of weakness. On the contrary, they believe that conforming to the group requires great self-discipline and is a sign of inner strength.

Why the Japanese should place so much emphasis on group solidarity is uncertain. But it may be a way of coping with one of the country's oldest problems — many people living in a limited amount of space. Overcrowded conditions make cooperation and personal restraint essential if life is to be tolerable. The Japanese seem to have found the answer in organized group activities.

Many young Japanese boys learn judo in large, well-organized groups.

Harmony. The virtue admired most by the Japanese is harmony, for the success of group life depends on it. When a group has to make a decision, it is essential that all the members accept it or, at least, that no one objects to it strongly. Decisions reached by a majority are not satisfactory — they leave too many people with the feeling that they are "losers." Decisions imposed by an individual, no matter how great his authority, would be resented even more.

Consensus. How does a group reach a decision that will be accepted almost unanimously? The Japanese system rests on lengthy discussions at which all members express their points of view. Suppose that some members of a group object to a new proposal. They must either persuade the others of the soundness of their objections, or else be persuaded themselves of the proposal's value. In any event, sharp confrontations must be avoided. Opinions are expressed cautiously, in language that is indirect and, perhaps, vague. Precise language may seem arrogant or threatening, but many thoughts can be communicated by implication. Eventually there is a meeting of minds. The proposal may be accepted or rejected, but the decision will be very nearly unanimous.

The process is time-consuming and, by American standards, extremely inefficient. American businessmen are often exasperated by the apparently endless negotiations that are required to make a deal with the Japanese. For the Japanese, however, the system is vital. It assures that all the members of a group will feel a sense of involvement with its decisions and will carry them out willingly.

Self-expression. Although the Japanese tend to subordinate their individuality to the group, they are far from being faceless robots. They still retain a strong sense of self-identity, which they are able to express in a variety of ways. Let us see what some of them are:

Hiking and mountain climbing are quite popular in Japan. This man is climbing Mount Fuji.

1. Most Japanese find personal fulfillment in their love of nature. Nature hikes and outings are extremely popular and provide needed respites from the pressures of society. Even at home the Japanese are reminded of nature in the tiny landscape gardens they cultivate, and in the art of flower arrangement.

2. Literally millions of Japanese express themselves by writing poetry, including the *tanka* and *haiku* forms. Poetry magazines and study groups are very popular. Each year there is a national *tanka* contest. The winning poems are read in the presence of the emperor, who contributes a poem of his own.

3. The majority of Japanese are skilled in at least one art, whether it is music, dancing, drama, or painting. There are numerous schools of instruction in both traditional and modern forms, and each one has a large number of devoted followers. The Japanese like to display their skills at parties. In one evening you might see a geisha-style dance, hear a recitation from a *No* drama, or watch a demonstration of calligraphy. All of these skills are, of course, a means of expressing self-identity.

Personality traits. The emphasis on group loyalty and harmony in Japanese society has done much to shape the personality of the people. On the surface, at least, they seem to be quite unemotional. They will rarely show affection in public, except toward young children. The tendency of Westerners to kiss or embrace openly seems very strange to the Japanese. They smile a good deal, but often to hide embarrassment or anger. They seldom raise their voices or scold. Among their friends they are polite to a fault. Recently, for example, a Japanese was asked whether an American he knew spoke the Japanese language well. "Tom?" he asked. "Oh yes, he speaks Japanese very well. Unfortunately, I understand very little of what he says."

The Japanese are a very formal people and observe thousands of rules of etiquette. They worry that they

Many Japanese people enjoy the art of flower arranging — perhaps because it can be done as part of a group or as a form of individual self-expression during quiet moments alone.

may not be doing the right thing, especially when they are outside their own familiar groups. In unfamiliar situations they are likely to become self-conscious and shy.

Japanese boys and girls seldom get together on a one-to-one basis. When they do they are usually quite ill at ease. This may account for the tendency of the girl to giggle, and for the boy to draw in his breath nervously, while conversing.

The difficulty that young Japanese have in making friends with the opposite sex has been the subject of numerous articles and works of fiction. In "The First Date," a short story by Atsuko Anzai,* a high school student asks a girl he has met for permission to write her a letter. She agrees. After a long wait a letter finally arrives at her home. It is as follows:

"When you gave me your permission, I wanted to write a letter right away. But when vacation came there were club meetings, I had to help my married sister move, and there was just no time to relax. No, it is more truthful to say that even when I had time I just couldn't write.

"This is the first time that I have ever written a letter to a girl asking to get better acquainted. I don't know how to go about it. If I make a slip, you might get mad. To tell the truth, I am scared.

"Ever since I first saw you at school last year, I have wanted to become your friend. There are lots of girls at school, but I have never met anyone like you. How can I put it? This is beginning to sound like flattery. I'm not doing well at all, but you just make me feel great. Well, I hope you don't think I'm some kind of a nut.

"If possible, I would like to have you come over to my house for a visit, or I could go wherever you say and we could have a long talk. But I wouldn't want it unless you did. Because I would be very happy if you would just let me write letters like this from time to time."

Status and rank. Class distinctions based on income are not strong in Japan because there are few extremes of wealth and poverty. Many Japanese are, however, very conscious of status and rank based on age, length of service in a company or government bureau, or leadership in a group. For them such distinctions are entirely natural. They see no reason why the aged should try to act young, or the president of a company should act like "one of the boys." Such behavior would seem extremely awkward to them.

The Japanese commonly show their respect for status by bowing. The higher a person's status, the deeper and longer are the bows that he or she will receive. In the family, aged parents receive not only the deepest bows, but the first dip in the bathtub and the seat of honor in the house. This seat is located at the opposite end of the entrance and in front of the *tokonoma*,* an alcove for art objects. On formal occasions the most honored guests also sit in this area. One result is that entrances frequently get jammed with people who, uncertain of their status, insist on sitting in the place of least honor.

The Japanese language has endless gradations of politeness that reflect status. Humble forms apply to oneself, while increasingly polite forms apply to people of higher status. A person who is admired for his wisdom is reverently addressed as *sensei*,* or teacher. Among men, a very close friend may be addressed as *kun*.* If his name is Tanaka he would be called Tanaka-kun.* Almost everyone else, male or female, single or married, is called *san*,* the equivalent of our Mr., Mrs., and Miss. If a person's name is Suzuki* he or she would be called Suzuki-san.* Except for children and intimate friends, people are almost never called by their first names.

San is also combined with nouns to designate status. For example: *okusan*,* the lady of the house, or *Shacho-san*,* Mr. Company President.

Like 90 percent of Japanese homes, this one has an electric vacuum cleaner. Note the use of Western furniture and carpets.

Attitudes toward women. From the feudal era until the 20th century, Japanese women were dominated by men. From childhood they were taught to believe that they owed complete obedience first to their fathers, then to their husbands, and in late life to their sons. A 17th-century Japanese textbook described a woman's duty to her husband in this fashion:

"A woman must think of her husband as her lord, and she must serve him reverently. . . . In her dealings with her husband, her facial expressions and her language should be courteous, humble, and yielding. She should never be peevish or obstinate, never rude or arrogant.

146

When her husband issues instructions, she must never disobey them. . . . A woman should look on her husband as if he were heaven itself.

"The five worst weaknesses of women are disobedience, unhappiness, slander, jealousy, and silliness. It is beyond doubt that seven or eight out of every 10 women have these weaknesses. That is why women are inferior to men. A woman should correct these weaknesses by self-inspection and self-criticism. . . . Women are so stupid that it is important for them always to distrust themselves and to obey their husbands."

The traditional Japanese housewife served her husband almost slavishly. As recently as the 1920's it was not uncommon to see her walking in the street laden down with young children and heavy bundles. Her husband strode before her majestically, unencumbered by any burdens. At home she was the first to get up in the morning, and the last to go to bed at night. She did not eat until she had served her husband, and then her children. The same order was followed for the evening bath.

If she was unhappy with the drudgery of her life, there was little she could do about it. Her husband could divorce her very easily, simply by erasing her name from the family register in the record office. For her, getting a divorce was almost impossible. If the husband divorced her he paid no alimony. Her opportunities for making a living were limited to work as a servant or a waitress. Her chances of getting another husband after the disgrace of a divorce were very slim.

Since the end of World War II, the status of women in Japan has improved considerably. Much of the improvement is due to Japan's postwar constitution which states: "There shall be no discrimination in political, economic, or social relations because of sex. . . . Marriage shall be maintained through mutual cooperation with the equal rights of husband and wife as a basis."

147

Although women such as this Tokyo office worker now make up 40 percent of Japan's work force, they do not get equal pay.

Today a Japanese wife and her husband usually walk side by side, and the chances are that *he* is carrying the babies and the bundles. If there is a family car she drives it almost as much as he does. And if there are dishes to be done in the evening, he may even volunteer to help.

In recent decades more and more women have taken jobs in business and industry. Today women comprise 40 percent of the entire work force. Among them are many teachers, doctors, and executives in small businesses. However, the great majority of women workers in Japan have low-status, service-oriented jobs. Many earn half as much as men for doing the same work. Often companies politely ask them to quit when they reach their late twenties. The companies argue that women aren't entitled to well-paid, success-oriented jobs, because they eventually marry, drop out, and have children.

However, this explanation is outmoded. Today 70 percent of working women are married, and many have children. Most of these are younger women. Unlike their mothers, they increasingly reject women's traditional roles in Japanese society. According to a poll taken in 1979, over 60 percent of Japanese women believe that competent women should be allowed to enter fields previously reserved for men.

They may soon get their wish. Already, due to a shortage of qualified male workers, women are being hired in the traditionally male-dominated field of computing.

Religion. As already noted, many Japanese no longer take their Buddhist and Shinto faiths very seriously. Buddhism began to decline during Tokugawa times when people became more concerned with the "here and now," and less concerned with the hereafter. Under the Meiji leaders, who stressed modernization, Buddhism declined even further.

Today there are still numerous Buddhist temples and monasteries in Japan, but few people come to worship at them. Some Buddhist practices survive, however. Most funerals are conducted by Buddhist priests, and the dead are usually buried in temple grounds after cremation. Many families still keep ancestral tablets, which they place on small Buddhist altars in the home.

As Japan became increasingly urbanized, Shinto, the native faith that centers on nature gods, also declined. During the Meiji Restoration, however, the government leaders favored Shinto because its ancient myths inspired reverence for the emperor. Until the end of World War II, state-supported Shinto was used to foster nationalistic pride and militarism.

The U.S. occupation ended the tie between Shinto and the state. Since then many Shinto shrines have fallen into decay for lack of funds. Some that are famous for the beauty of their natural surroundings are still vis-

ited by eager sightseers. But these visits have little, if any, religious significance. Shinto survives today mainly in wedding ceremonies and in annual shrine festivals that give the Japanese an opportunity to wear traditional clothes and celebrate boisterously.

Christianity was legalized by Japan's Meiji rulers in 1873. Today it has about 750,000 adherents, fairly evenly divided between Protestants and Catholics. Although they comprise less than one percent of the total population, their influence in Japanese life has been significant. Christians have played a major role in education and social work, and are widely admired as people of high moral principles. During the yule season Japanese department stores enthusiastically display Christmas decorations and play Christmas carols.

In recent decades a number of new religions have sprung up in Japan. Most of them appeal to people who feel isolated by the impersonality of modern industrial society. They offer members many social activities and the hope of finding happiness and prosperity in the near future. The largest of the new religions is Soka Gakkai,* which has about six million members. Soka Gakkai emphasizes absolute faith and immediate worldly benefits. "If you sincerely wish for something hard enough," the movement proclaims, "you will surely receive it."

During Tokugawa times Japanese society was dominated by Confucian thought. Confucianism in Japan was not a religion — it had no deities and no priesthood. As a philosophy it emphasized the need for harmonious living, ethical conduct, and proper etiquette. Today few Japanese think of themselves as Confucianists, yet most of them are still strongly influenced by Confucian concepts in their everyday behavior.

Top left: The midsummer Gion festival in Kyoto reenacts a feudal parade to please the Shinto gods. Bottom: a Soka Gakkai meeting in a Tokyo suburb.

Double-check

Review

1. Other than the family, what group is the most important in Japan?

2. What do the Japanese believe group conformity requires and shows?

3. List three factors which can determine status and rank in Japan.

4. What is responsible for much of the improvement in the status of Japanese women since World War II?

5. As a philosophy in Japan, what did Confucianism emphasize the need for?

Discussion

1. A Jesuit priest visiting Japan wrote in 1580: "The people are . . . courteous and highly civilized, so much so that they surpass all other known races of the world. . . . On the other hand, they are the most false and treacherous people . . . for from childhood they are taught never to reveal their hearts." Based on information in this and previous chapters, do you agree with this statement? Why, or why not?

2. What reasons — historical, social, religious, or others — might explain why most Japanese tend to be intensely group-oriented and frown on individualism? How do these attitudes compare with American attitudes on such matters? What factors might explain American values?

3. The Japanese constitution states: "There shall be no discrimination in political, economic, or social relations because of sex. . . . Marriage shall be maintained through mutual cooperation with the equal rights of husband and wife as a basis." Would you rather be a man or a woman in postwar Japanese society? Give reasons for your answer.

Activities

1. Some students might role-play conversations in which they express their anger at a friend in the American way and then in the Japanese way.

2. The class might try to reach a decision on a sticky subject in the Japanese manner — by consensus — unanimously, if possible. How long does it take? How do the participants feel about the matter afterward? Could such a method become practice in the U.S.? Give reasons for your answers.

3. Some students might write the girl's reply — Japanese style — to the high school student's letter in the story "The First Date." Other students might translate the boy's letter into a version that might be written by a young man in the United States. Then others could write a U.S. girl's reply.

Skills

For the building of a new Japan
Let's put our strength and mind together
Doing our best to promote production
Sending our goods to the people of the world
Endlessly and continuously
Like water gushing from a fountain
Grow industry, grow, grow, grow!
Harmony and sincerity!
Matsushita Electric!

— *Matsushita Electric Company Song*

Use the passage above and information in Chapter 7 to answer the following questions.

1. Who do you think probably sings this song?
(a) Matsushita's president
(b) Matsushita's stockholders
(c) Matsushita's workers

2. Judging from the first line of the song, when was the song most likely to have been written?
(a) during feudal times
(b) during World War II
(c) after World War II

3. What do the people who sing this song want to do about production?
(a) end it   (b) increase it   (c) turn it into water

4. What Japanese characteristic is represented by this song?

Chapter 8

Family

How do young Japanese feel about arranged marriages today? As teenagers it is not uncommon for them to insist they will choose their own mates. Yet a surprisingly large number of them will later accept marriage partners chosen for them by other people, especially by their parents.

Marriage, traditional-style. Before the 20th century, the practice of arranged marriages was unquestioned. Typically the parents of an eligible daughter would ask a relative or a friend to find a suitable husband for her. The use of go-betweens had advantages. A go-between could praise the daughter more than proper etiquette would permit the parents. In addition, both families had to ask blunt questions about the wealth and social standing of the other. These questions often aroused bitter feelings. The use of go-betweens assured that there would be no angry confrontations between the families.

If the parents on both sides were satisfied that the proposed match was a good one, the young couple was introduced at a formal meeting of the families. The feelings of the young man and woman toward each other were considered, but generally the couple was expected to obey

154

their parents' wishes. If no serious obstacles arose, the families would then proceed to make all the marriage arrangements. Until the wedding, the young couple would not see each other again. It was believed, or hoped, that love would develop after the marriage.

Marriage today. Young people today no longer feel obliged to marry partners chosen by their parents, yet many of them willingly accept their parents' guidance. As we have seen, Japanese boys and girls tend to socialize in groups, and are quite shy in one-to-one situations. As a result, young Japanese often lack confidence in their ability to choose appropriate marriage partners and look to their parents for help. A first meeting between a young man and woman is still commonly arranged by their parents. And it is still common for the parents to employ go-betweens to investigate family backgrounds.

Some Japanese also depend on their friends to introduce them to suitable partners. In addition, computer dating services have grown increasingly popular in the last few years. Some large companies even have their own private dating services for their employees.

On their dates the young man and woman discuss their views about marriage and children, their goals, and their interests. If after a few dates, the couple feel that they are personally compatible, they may become engaged. Marriage follows fairly soon. A long courtship, it is feared, might lead to doubts that would interfere with their future happiness. If they are not compatible they will break up. Then they will wait for their parents, friends, or dating service to introduce them to others.

Does the system work? Statistics indicate that the great majority of Japanese marriages are enduring. Only one Japanese marriage out of 25 ends in divorce, compared with one out of three in the United States.

A Shinto wedding. Most Japanese are married in a traditional Shinto ceremony. The bride usually wears a kimono and a white headress called a *tsuno-katushi,** or

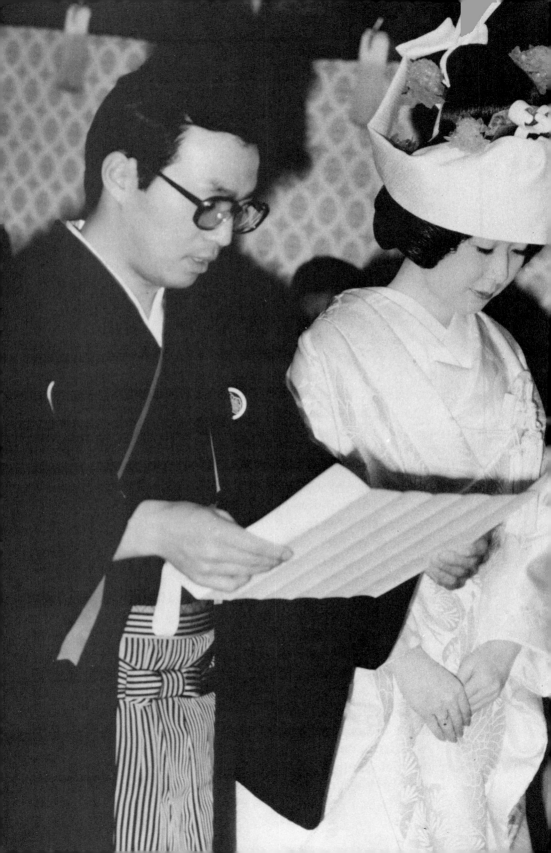

Modern Shinto weddings combine old and new.
Note the Western style of dress (left and above)
and the traditional sansankudo (above).

horns of jealousy, and it signifies that the bride will never be jealous of her husband. The groom almost always wears Western-style clothes. Many grooms favor a cutaway, a formal coat with tails in the back. The high point of the ceremony is the *sansankudo,** when the bride and groom each take three sips from three cups of *sake** (rice wine).

After the wedding there is a reception and dinner at which numerous toasts are drunk. Later the guests approach the newlyweds one by one, bow, and offer wishes for future harmony, fertility, and prosperity. When the guests leave they are given presents to take home with them, usually a package of food or a piece of lacquerware. October and November are the most popular months for getting married, for then the honeymooners can enjoy the brilliant colors of autumn foliage.

Traditional wives. Japanese wives generally have more independence than they did in the past. The old saying, "When the husband calls, the woman jumps," no longer holds true. Today the typical husband is considerate of his wife's feelings and genuinely wishes to be liked by her. As a rule, he does not give orders or take advantage of his authority.

Lately, the behavior of Japanese wives falls into two general patterns—traditional and modern. This is usually determined by their age, education, and work experience. More traditional wives tend to be middle-aged or older. If they are educated, they often went to schools that were inferior to those attended by their brothers. If they worked, they quit when their children were born. In marriage, their husbands enjoy a higher status and greater prestige. Typically, a husband may call his wife by her first name, but she does not reciprocate. Instead, she may call him *otochan*,* or father. When he arrives home at night he gets plenty of attention. His wife hastens to make him comfortable, to feed him, and to draw his bath. If he decides to spend an evening out, that is his privilege. His wife will not ask where he has been.

Traditionally, Japanese men work long hours and go out in the evenings and on weekends with their male friends. If they spend little time with their families, traditional wives do not complain. In mixed gatherings the traditional wife does not speak unless she is spoken to. As a rule, she will agree with her husband's opinions rather than express opinions of her own. If she has any grown sons who still live with the family, she will treat them with a similar, though lesser, deference.

Although the traditional husband's authority is greater than his wife's, she usually considers the household her domain and seeks to run it her own way. Usually she manages most of the household finances. Her husband gives her his paychecks, and she gives him a daily allowance. However, she always consults him when large purchases are made, and she has no legal rights over the family money.

Basically the technique of the traditional wife is to please her husband as much as possible so that he will willingly accept her management of the home. She studies his character and understands his moods. She knows when to humor him, and when to leave him alone. She avoids criticizing him or offending his pride. If he should become angry with her, she will rarely defend herself. Instead she will accuse herself of being inadequate and try even harder to please him.

Modern wives. Whether out of necessity or the desire to have a career, many women contine to work after they marry. Some try to pick husbands who will be supportive and understanding of this. Usually these couples are in their twenties and thirties, but sometimes they are older. Their relationship often includes sharing many of the household responsibilities. Some married men are learning to cook for their families, which may shock their traditional mothers and fathers.

If a wife does the cooking, she is just as likely to cook her own favorite dishes as her husband's. She calls him by his first name and in general defers to him less than a more traditional wife would. In these less traditional families, men are beginning to spend more time with their families in the evenings and on weekends. As a result, they play a larger role in disciplining and teaching the children.

The mother-in-law problem. Before the modern era, when a woman married she went to live with her husband's family. She was expected to learn its customs and to prove by hard work and submissiveness that she was worthy of being accepted. Primarily she had to prove herself to her mother-in-law by obeying her every wish. If she failed, she was sent back to her original home in disgrace. In most cases divorces were initiated by the mother-in-law rather than the husband. Modern Japanese women are very aware of the power of this old tradition.

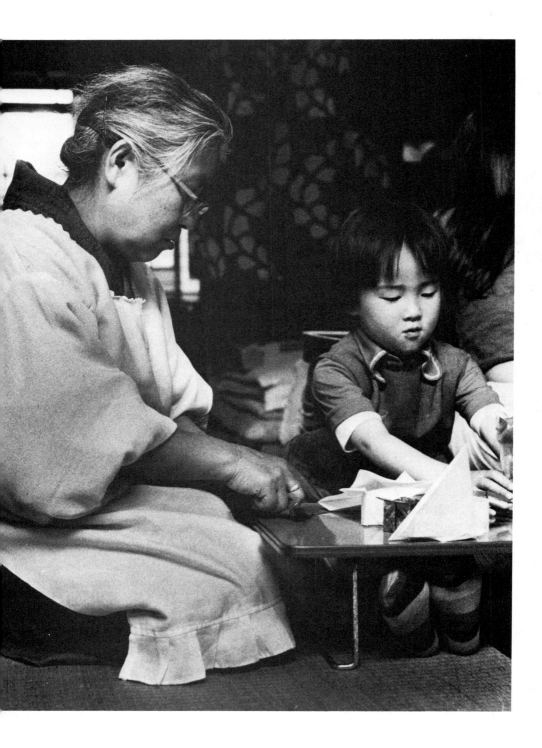

To share a home with their husband's mother means that they will probably find it difficult to run the household in their own way.

Today most Japanese women still shudder at the prospect of living with a mother-in-law. Yet it is sometimes impossible to avoid, either because of economic circumstances, or because the husband's sense of duty obliges him to offer his mother a home with the couple. When the wife and mother-in-law do live together, there are likely to be serious tensions between them. Ideally, the wife is still supposed to yield to her mother-in-law's wishes. In reality, however, she often resents attempts by the mother-in-law to supervise her.

Disputes about how the children should be raised are common. The wife is likely to believe that her mother-in-law's ideas about raising children are old-fashioned and superstitious. She tends to rely on more modern information that she gets from reading newpapers, magazines, and books. Her mother-in-law may not deny the value of this information, but is more likely to believe that experience and customs count for more. She, after all, has already raised a family.

Usually the husband tries to stay out of any dispute between his wife and his mother. But if the situation becomes intolerable he may have to settle it by taking sides. He may support either his wife or his mother, but in either case his opinion is decisive. Unfortunately, a new dispute is likely to arise before long. As long as tradition clashes with modern ways, the rivalry between a Japanese wife and her mother-in-law is likely to continue.

Raising the young. When a traditional Japanese mother has to go out shopping, she will rarely trust a baby-sitter to care for her young child. Instead, she will strap

Modern mothers-in-law help with children at home and elsewhere. Left: A grandmother teaches the traditional art of paper folding.

the child to her back and carry it with her. Even in the home she seldom lets the child out of her sight. Cribs and playpens are almost unknown in Japan. When the mother does housework, she keeps the child close by.

The Japanese believe that close physical contact is a natural form of affection and to deprive children of it is cruel. Often a Japanese child sleeps with its mother from infancy to the birth of another child. Then the new baby sleeps with the mother. The mother and father also bathe with their young children and sometimes use the occasion to have heart-to-heart talks with them.

In few societies are the ties between a mother and her children as close as they are in Japan. A Japanese mother tends to lavish attention and affection on her youngsters. She crawls on the floor with them and lets them climb on her back. She knows all kinds of ways to entertain them, including little hand exercises, songs with gestures, animal imitations, and peek-a-boo games. She allows them a great many liberties and rarely spanks them or even criticizes them.

Most mothers are quicker to gratify the wishes of a son than a daughter. For many years Japanese mothers have believed that boys are more impulsive than girls and are likely to become uncontrollable if denied anything. Girls have traditionally been credited with being more patient and better able to accept deprivation. However, these beliefs may change as Japanese sex roles change.

A Japanese father also tends to be very kind and gentle toward his children. He too will play with them on the floor when he is home. They do not feel as free with him, however, as with their mother. No matter how mild or good-natured he may be, they are aware of him as someone with authority. Respect for his authority is instilled in them primarily by the mother. It is she who warns them that they must humor him, or that he will punish them if they do poorly in school. In fact, however, the father rarely disciplines them. He leaves such matters almost entirely to their mother.

Techniques of discipline. By American standards many Japanese children are pampered and overprotected. How, then, can one account for their good manners and disciplined behavior by the time they enter school? By lavishing affection on her children the traditional Japanese mother establishes a very close relationship with them. This tends to make them cooperative and responsive to her wishes. When the time comes for her to teach them proper behavior she has little difficulty in getting them to comply. Generally the children *want* to do what she tells them, especially when she praises them with words like o-riko* (nice child) and *jozu** (skillful).

If the children are uncooperative, the mother has other techniques for getting them to obey. She may tell them, for example, that if they do not behave correctly, other people will laugh at them. The children dread being shamed by the outside world and will do their utmost to avoid it. The mother may also warn them of punishment by their father, or even by supernatural forces like ghosts. Her last resort may be to threaten to leave them alone outside the house, a prospect that is truly frightening to them.

Generally, however, the traditional Japanese mother believes that keeping her children happy and flattering them gets better results than fear. Physical punishment is almost unthinkable to her. The sight of a child being spanked or yelled at in public shocks her.

How successful is the Japanese mother with her techniques of gentle persuasion? Most U.S. observers find that Japanese school children are generally quiet and well-behaved, polite to their teachers and other adults, and considerate toward each other.

Yet the practice of indulging children in their early years does create difficulties for them later on. Many Jap-

Japanese school children do not always dress so formally, but they are generally quiet and well-behaved.

anese children become unusually dependent on their parents—especially their mothers—for affection and security. Away from home they are often frightened and unable to make decisions for themselves. As they grow older dependence on their parents may be transferred to their school and work groups. Their need for approval tends to make them readily accept the authority of the group. The fear instilled in them by their mothers that they will be laughed at if they do not behave correctly remains a powerful force for conformity.

The great devotion of traditional Japanese mothers to their children can also create problems for the mothers in later life. When the children grow up and leave home a Japanese mother sometimes feels quite useless. Often she has sacrificed a great deal for them and has a limited social life and few interests outside the home. She may wish to go back to school, but there are few opportunities for re-entry education in Japanese universities. If she wishes to work, it may be difficult for her to find a job, especially if she wants a full-time job. If she becomes a widow and none of the children offers her a home, she may talk nostalgically about the past, when parents were welcomed by the married children and obeyed in everything. Yet her own attitudes may have changed with the times, and it is doubtful whether she would want to restore the past, even if it were possible.

Because some Japanese mothers work, they need someone to care for their children. Because women generally earn less than men and the status of men is higher, it would be unthinkable for a husband to stay home to do housework and care for the children. To fill the gap, many day-care centers have opened up, especially in the cities. Twenty thousand centers are in operation in Japan. It is estimated that one in five Japanese children under the age of six is in day-care. Many people in Japan think that this is bad for children. They say that children in day-care do not learn the Japanese language, value system, and art as well as children cared for solely by their mothers. Despite this criticism, the demand for day-care increases every year.

Perhaps one of the most significant changes in the Japanese family is its size. In the early 20th century, the average Japanese woman had five children and died in her forties. Today Japanese women usually have no more than two children, and live an average of 30 years longer.

165

Even on shopping trips Japanese babies are never far from their mothers — unless they're in dreamland.

Thus, women in Japan have far more time on their hands, and many of them want to use that time productively.

Beware of strangers. Most Japanese, as we have seen, feel comfortable within their familiar groups but are usually ill at ease among strangers. Strangers, in fact, are often viewed with distrust and suspicion. A well-known Japanese proverb illustrates this attitude: "If you meet a stranger, regard him as a robber."

The distrust of strangers is apparent in the way the Japanese carefully guard the privacy of their homes. The typical suburban home is surrounded by a high fence, and for further protection there may be a watchdog. The fence gate is kept locked most of the time and can be opened only from the inside. It is opened for errand boys, but they do not enter the house. Visitors remain at the door of the house until they are invited to enter. Most Japanese prefer that their homes remain unknown to outsiders. Many take comfort from the fact that their houses are seldom numbered consecutively and therefore are difficult to find.

Other than relatives or very close friends, guests are rarely invited to a Japanese home. Should casual friends or business acquaintances be invited, they are usually confined to one room. It is almost inconceivable for the hosts to take them on a tour of the entire home, as Americans often do. The Japanese not only value the privacy of their homes, they would consider it in poor taste to show off their possessions to others.

The Japanese home. By American standards, traditional Japanese homes are uncomfortable. They are built of very light materials and are intended to let in as much air and sunlight as possible. Walls are often made of balsa wood and paper panels. They slide open or can be removed entirely. This may be very pleasant in the summertime. But in the winter these houses are drafty. Most of Japan enjoys mild winters, and for a long time central heating was considered a luxury. Often the only heat came from the *kotatsu,** a small pit in the floor of one room that

Before the arrival of central heating, most Japanese kept warm around a kotatsu like this.

contains a charcoal-burning or electric *hibachi.** A low table covered the kotatsu, and a quilt was stretched over the table and the surrounding area. During the winter the family ate, read, talked, and watched TV around the kotatsu, their feet inside it, their laps covered by the quilt.

As a heating device the kotatsu is very limited, so the Japanese have found other ways to keep warm. They take long, steaming-hot baths in a tub that is shorter, but deeper, than American bathtubs. They drink hot tea often. They sleep on thick, heavy cotton mattresses called *futons** that they stretch out on the floor. Then they cover themselves with quilts and huddle close together for additional comfort.

A typical home is quite small and cramped. Around Tokyo it averages less than 200 square feet. It includes an entranceway, where shoes are exchanged for slippers, and five rooms that are connected by a hall. Two of the rooms are covered with straw mats called *tatami*.* The tatami stays clean for a long time because nobody ever tracks in dirt from outside. These rooms are used for eating, sleeping, and entertaining guests. (During the day the bedding is folded up and stored in a closet.) These two rooms adjoin each other and can be made into one by sliding open, or removing, the doors between them.

As in other areas of Japanese life, Western customs have taken hold. Central heating has eliminated the need for the kotatsu in many homes. Higher, Western-style tables and chairs have followed. Floors are covered with rugs and carpets instead of tatami.

Compared with those in the U.S., Japanese kitchens are ususally tiny and inconvenient. It usually contains a two-burner gas stove, an electric rice cooker, and a small refrigerator. The Japanese believe in keeping the bathroom and the toilet separated. One reason may be that until recently few homes had flush toilets and modern sewage systems. That too has changed.

Housekeeping. Because the Japanese home is usually small and furnished rather sparingly, it is relatively easy to care for. Futons, for example, can be folded up and stored in a closet in much less time than it takes to make an equivalent number of beds in an American home. Modern electric appliances have also simplified Japanese housework. For example, more than 90 percent of Japanese households have vacuum cleaners. The house has no lawn to speak of, and the garden is so small it requires little tending.

Other than caring for the children, the principle housework is the preparation and serving of food. Because the kitchen has no oven, most meals are prepared simply and quickly. Rice is still the main food, and it is very easy to prepare with an electric cooker. Vegetables such as cucumbers, radishes, eggplant, cabbage, and gourds can be

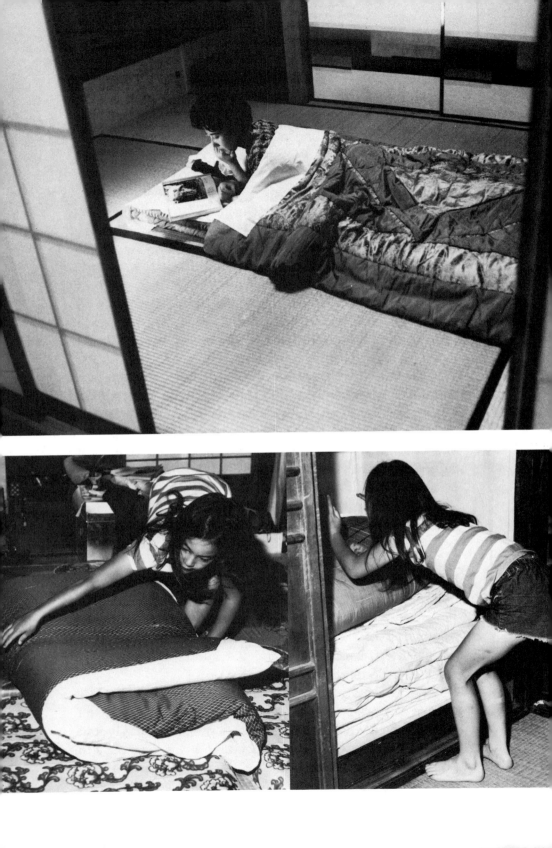

bought pickled and ready to serve. Or they may be pickled at home in vats of brine. Other vegetables are cooked in oil for only a minute or two over a very hot fire.

Fish is eaten raw, sun-dried, fried, or broiled. The most popular soup in Japan is *miso-shuru*,* which is standard breakfast fare. It is prepared with boiling water, a few dried sardines for stock, and about half a cup of bean paste. Vendors still come to most neighborhoods selling noodles and sweet potatoes that are kept warm by heated rocks. Desserts are plain, usually a piece of fresh fruit or a bowl of rice with hot tea poured over it.

Recently, Western-style food has become a popular alternative in Japan. Hamburgers and other fast foods are popular. Because it is usually imported, beef is costly, and therefore is considered a great delicacy. For dessert, the Japanese have recently discovered Western-style ice cream and chocolate-chip cookies.

Who will take care of the Japanese home and children in the future? With more career opportunities slowly opening up for Japanese women, it is possible that the traditional, submissive, Japanese housewife will become a rare creature. This will certainly cause many changes in Japanese family life, especially in childcare and the relationships between husbands and wives. Already, the Japanese family has begun to adapt to a changing world.

Top left: A Tokyo woman reads before sleeping on a futon in a typically spare, uncluttered room. Bottom: Futons are easily folded and stored out of sight during the day.

Double-check

Review

1. How has the tradition of arranged marriages in Japan changed? How has it stayed the same? Why?

2. What was the traditional relationship between wives and mothers-in-law? What is one major issue on which a wife and her mother-in-law are likely to disagree today?

3. What new method of child care has come about as a result of the increase of mothers who work outside the home? What percentage of children under six are affected?

4. What is the traditional Japanese attitude toward strangers? How does it affect the way visitors are entertained?

5. How do Japanese houses differ from those in the West? How does this make housekeeping simple?

Discussion

1. What are the advantages and disadvantages of arranged marriages? Which system do you prefer? Why?

2. What are some major differences between American and Japanese husband-wife relationships? Who, if anyone, is more dominant in American husband-wife relationships? Should men and women have different amounts of authority? Explain your answers.

3. The Japanese have a system of rearing children that is, in many ways, different from most Americans'. In what major ways is it different? How close should parents be to their children? Decide if you would prefer the Japanese or American way and state why.

Activities

1. A committee of students might research the traditional Japanese diet and how it has influenced the health of the Japanese people. What diseases occur less often in Japan than the U.S.? What diseases occur more often? How is this related to nutrition? Students might discuss the recent changes in the Japanese diet and speculate how these changes might affect the national health.

2. After researching the topic, a group of students might role-play a scene showing how Japanese marriages were arranged. Characters would include a go-between, a girl and her parents, and a boy and his parents.

Skills

PERCENTAGES OF HOUSEHOLDS
BY NUMBER OF MEMBERS

Number	1930	1955	1960	1965	1970
1	5.5	3.5	5.2	8.1	10.8
2	11.7	10.8	12.7	14.3	15.4
3	14.8	14.5	15.9	18.2	19.7
4	15.1	16.6	18.7	22.3	25.5
5	14.5	16.7	17.1	16.2	14.5
6	12.7	14.1	13.1	10.6	8.5
7	9.9	10.3	8.5	6.1	3.5
8	6.8	6.5	4.6	2.5	1.4
9	4.1	3.6	2.3	1.1	0.5
10	2.4	1.9	1.1	0.4	0.2
11 or more	2.5	1.6	0.8	0.3	0.1
Average	4.98	4.97	4.54	4.05	3.69

Source: *Japanese Society Today*, Tadashi Fukutake

Use the table above and information in Chapter 8 to answer the following questions.

1. What do the numbers on the left of the table stand for?

2. Is the number of people in the average Japanese household increasing or decreasing?

3. In what year did 9.9 percent of Japanese households have seven people living in them? What percent of Japanese households had seven people in them in 1970?

4. Which type of household (according to the number of people living in it) almost doubled between 1930 and 1970? Which type was the same percentage of households in both years?

5. Roughly how many square feet per person are there in the average household in a typical Tokyo home?

Chapter 9

Education

IN FEBRUARY 1979, 18-year-old Toshio Hashimoto* received the telegram he had been waiting for so anxiously. It was much too important for him to open alone. He waited until both his parents were at his side. Then, with trembling hands, he removed the telegram from its envelope and read the message: "The cherry blossoms are falling." Toshio turned pale and dropped the telegram.

His mother's eyes filled with tears as she asked, "How can we tell our friends?"

Toshio's father said, "Leave that to me. I will tell them." Then he said to his son, "Don't worry. It's not the end of the world. Next year you will do better."

"The cherry blossoms are falling" was a coded message designed to soften, if possible, its impact. It meant that Toshio had failed to pass the entrance examination for Tokyo University, Japan's top college. A year of intensive studying, during which Toshio had given up movies, athletics, hobbies, and all other recreation, had been in vain. Now he would have to cram day and night for another year and hope to pass the entrance examination next year. If he failed again, he would probably try for a lesser college or give up the idea of going to college altogether.

The key to success. For Toshio the prospect of not being accepted by any college was almost unendurable. In no other society does a successful career in business or government depend so much on educational achievements as it does in Japan. The best companies and most important government bureaus recruit the graduates of the top-ranking colleges and virtually assure them lifetime jobs with steady advancement. Those who graduate from other colleges usually settle for lesser jobs, but they too can count on security and white-collar status. As a result, almost every student who is ambitious for success seeks to enter college. Unfortunately the number of candidates for college entrance far exceeds the number that can be accepted. Only two of every five applicants make it. The rate is even lower for those who seek admission to top-ranking colleges — one of every six.

In Japan the best colleges are the national universities. They charge only nominal fees and are much less expensive to attend than a private college. Entrance is based on merit rather than social status or ability to pay.

Education in Japan is compulsory through junior high school. Students who wish to continue their educations must pass stiff entrance examinations both for senior high school and college. The competition to enter senior high schools is almost as fierce as it is for colleges. This is especially true of high schools that are noted for the high proportion of their graduates who gain admission to the top colleges.

Some Japanese schools are closely connected to each other from level to level. A child who enters one of these "escalator" schools at the kindergarten level has a good chance of progressing all the way to the university level. The number of applicants is so great, however, that kindergarten entrance examinations must be given. Even then not all who pass can be accepted. The final selection is made by lottery.

There's not much talking in the Tokyo public library.

Examination hell. Because acceptance by good schools is crucial to a successful career, the pressure on students to pass entrance examinations is enormous. The Japanese call it "examination hell." It is believed to contribute to the relatively high suicide rate in Japan among teenagers and those in their early twenties.

Let us see how a typical junior high school student, whom we shall call Masao,* goes through the period of "examination hell." Masao begins to prepare for senior high school entrance examinations at least one year before they are given. (He may take examinations for as many as three or four schools, provided, of course, that they are not given on the same day.)

Masao spends several hours a day studying after school. During the summer vacation he devotes even more time to it. His mother constantly rides herd on him, for no one is more anxious for his success than she. She consults with Masao's teacher frequently and investigates several senior high schools to see which of them would be best for her son. She discusses them at length with her husband and Masao. Together they narrow the list to perhaps three choices.

January is the month when school applications are made and the "examination season" begins. Now almost everyone in Japan gets caught up in the excitement. Television news programs show applicants standing on line. Experts appear on talk shows to give advice to parents. TV commercials advertise guidebooks to help students pass examinations. Newspapers and magazines report on the records of high schools in advancing students to college. On street corners, in shops, and at dinner the upcoming examinations are the main topics of conversation.

One day in January Masao's mother will make her first application for his admission to a senior high school. (Only students who are candidates for college apply on their own.) If she is very zealous she may stand on line all night before the school opens. Actually the time of her arrival makes no difference, but she hopes that by being among the first on line she will make a favorable impression on the school officials. At any rate, she will not have to wait long once the school does open. Mothers who arrive at six o'clock in the morning may have to wait hours to apply, because by then the line will already be long. Masao's mother will have to go through the same procedure at each school to which she applies.

In the month before the examinations are given, Masao spends even more time cramming than he did before. At this time his brothers and sisters will relieve him of his household chores. His mother may bring him his meals on a tray, sharpen his pencils, and be ever ready to serve him. If the family can afford it, a tutor will come to the house regularly to help Masao. If not, Masao's father may come home early from work to help him.

Everyone walks on tiptoe in order not to disturb the young scholar. All social visiting comes to a halt.

In February the examinations begin. Masao's mother or father will accompany him to each one that he takes. There is a waiting room in the school where parents can sit while the examinations are in progress. As a rule the examinations consist mostly of multiple-choice questions and test the students' ability to memorize facts.

The results are posted. Several days pass before the results are announced. Usually the names, or code names, of successful candidates are posted on bulletin boards at the schools. Crowds of anxious parents and children begin to gather around the schools 24 hours in advance. When the results are put up, some people fear to look. They may wait several hours before they gather the courage to check the lists.

If Masao has succeeded, he and his parents will be all smiles and will tell their friends with great satisfaction. If he has failed, however, they will be terribly gloomy. Everyone will understand the reason and not question them. Masao's mother may stay at home for days and cry. When she does go out of the house it will be very difficult for her to face her friends.

Some Japanese parents use almost any means to get their children accepted by schools. Most schools, for example, have a few openings for students who do not pass the examinations. A committee of school officials screens the candidates and makes the final selections. Parents of failed students may appeal to influential friends to help sway the committee. Or they may bring gifts to important members of the committee. Although many school officials announce that they will not accept presents, it is sometimes difficult for them to refuse. The parents usually go to a great deal of trouble to buy unique gifts, and always present them very politely. Some school officials cannot help feeling obligated to these parents.

Japanese students are taught to pay careful attention to their work and their teachers.

The "education mama." A typical Japanese mother is known as an "education mama" because she is so ambitious for her children to succeed in school. She wants them to succeed not only for their sake, but also for her own. To a great extent she holds herself responsible for their performance in school, and the community shares this attitude. If her children do well she will be praised by teachers, friends, and neighbors. Her standing in the community will rise. If her children do poorly her image as an "education mama" will suffer, and her standing in the community will fall.

An "education mama" is both an assistant teacher and a hard taskmaster. Starting with the first grade her children are given homework that is often too difficult for them to do without her help. Sometimes the homework is not easy for her either, because many changes have

179

taken place in teaching since she went to school. In order to prepare herself she studies at home and often consults with her children's teachers. Keeping one step ahead of her children is a challenge that she takes seriously. During summer vacations her children are required to work on special projects that are handed in when school reopens. Like so many other "education mamas," she will probably do most of these projects herself.

Such a mother's reputation as a tutor is likely to be well-known in the community. At PTA meetings, for example, she may be openly praised or criticized (in the mild Japanese manner) by teachers, depending on how well her children are doing in school. On certain days she and other mothers are required to observe their children perform in the classroom. The teacher evaluates each child's performance aloud, directing her comments to the mother. It will be clear to all whether or not the mother has succeeded in her role as an assistant teacher.

A typical Japanese mother pushes her children hard to do well in school, but she also pushes herself hard and makes many sacrifices for them. At examination time she shares their excitement and anxiety. Their success will be her greatest reward; their failure, her greatest sorrow.

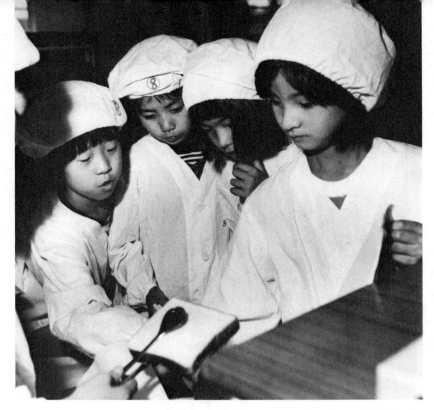

Left: A kindergarten class visits Meiji Outer Gardens, Tokyo's largest park. Above: lunch-time helpers. Below: Students help each other.

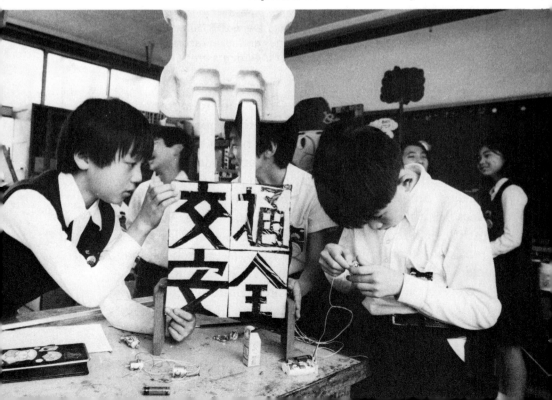

Junior high students at Tamagawa Gakuen private school learn English with the help of earphones and tape recordings. Dress and seating arrangements are rather formal.

The school system. Since the Meiji Restoration the Japanese government has stressed the importance of education to the development of the nation. The Ministry of Education regularly compares Japan's level of educational achievement with that of other nations and is not satisfied unless it ranks at or near the top. It constantly pressures the schools to raise their standards. While the quality of education in the United States varies greatly from one community to another, Japanese schools have achieved a remarkably uniform level of excellence.

By comparison with the United States, education in Japan is generally more demanding. The school day is longer, the school week is 5½ days, and the summer va-

182

cation is little more than a month. Discipline in the schools is strict, and daily homework is assigned from the first grade on. Large numbers of students at every level receive outside tutoring or attend after-class academies. All students are expected to study a foreign language, generally English, in junior high school. Math students are expected to complete calculus in high school. The Japanese probably absorb more formal education on the average than people of any other nation.

The competition among Japanese high schools — both for applicants and to place graduates in universities — is intense. Just as an American football coach is judged by the number of games his team wins, the Japanese high school principal is judged by the number of graduating students who go on to the top universities. The principal, in turn, judges his teachers by the same standard.

The teachers. Japanese teachers generally have more demands made on them than teachers in the United States. Even during summer vacations they are required to come to school at least two or three times to evaluate the progress of summer homework assignments and to supervise children's play activities. They are held responsible for their students' behavior inside and outside school. In school they must see that girls do not wear makeup, that they have simple hairdos, and that they wear the proper uniforms. In some private schools teachers must also see that boys and girls do not socialize with each other. If a Japanese child becomes a delinquent the teacher must share the blame. Some teachers spend a major part of their time helping children who have gotten into trouble in the community.

Most Japanese teachers do everything possible to help their students pass entrance examinations and commonly give them extra tutoring. The students' mothers have great respect for these teachers and often reward them with presents.

Once they get into college many students find time for political activities such as this demonstration against rising costs.

After the exams. Apart from entrance examinations, competition in Japanese schools is limited. Grades are not given much importance, and differences in ability are played down. Hardly anyone is ever "flunked out." Once students are admitted to a school, rivalry is subordinated to loyalty and friendship within the group.

Students who pass the entrance examinations to top universities often become apathetic or restless afterward. This is due, in part, to the psychological letdown they feel after so many years of intensive preparation. Many show little interest in their studies and devote themselves chiefly to sports, hobbies, or radical political activities. Radical activism is especially strong during the first two years when, at times, students may become openly rebellious. After this they usually settle down to prepare for the next round of examinations that they will take to enter the business world or government service. We will read about this in the next chapter.

Double-check

Review

1. What did the coded message, "The cherry blossoms are falling," mean to Toshio Hashimoto?

2. How does the Japanese attitude about the importance of education compare with that of other societies?

3. Why is a typical Japanese mother known as an "education mama"?

4. How does education in Japan compare with education in the U.S.?

5. Apart from entrance examinations, how is competition handled in Japanese schools?

Discussion

1. The pressure to gain admission to top schools fills a Japanese student's life from the kindergarten to the university level. Admission depends on repeatedly passing stiff entrance exams, which primarily test the ability to memorize facts. Do you think such examinations should have so much importance? How else might potential students be selected?

2. Japanese students have difficulty getting into schools, but once in, they don't face much competition for grades and usually don't have to worry about failing. How is the American system different? What are the advantages and drawbacks of each system? Which do you prefer? Why?

3. How is the role of Japanese parents — especially the "education mama" — different from that of American parents? Should parents be responsible for their children's performance in school? Why, or why not?

Activities

1. Two groups of students might imagine that they are Japanese students and write letters to friends. The first group has just passed the entrance exams for Tokyo University. The second group has failed the exams for the second time. After hearing the letters read aloud, the class might discuss them and choose the most realistic ones for posting on the bulletin board.

2. Several students might role-play Japanese parents, standing in line to apply for their children's admission to senior high school. The characters might discuss their children's talents and what the upcoming tests will mean to the children and to themselves. The scene could be serious or comic.

3. After being given a chance to read this chapter, your school principal might speak to the class about her or his views of Japanese education.

Skills

The Literacy Rate in Japan and 4 other nations: 1981

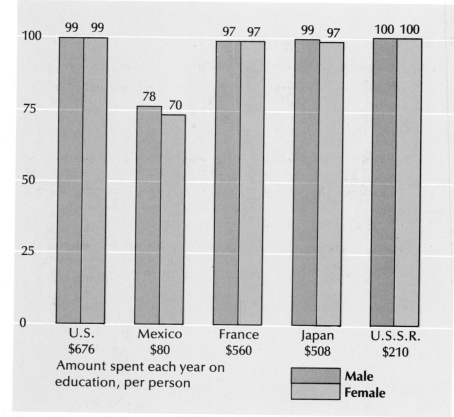

Source: The New Book of World Rankings, 1984

1. Where did the information in this graph come from? What year does it cover?

2. What do the numbers on top of the dark bars mean? What do those on top of the light bars mean?

3. Which country had the most literate women?

4. Which countries spent more on education per person than Japan? Which country spent the least money per person? Which country had the highest literacy rate?

Chapter 10

Business

BEHIND THE INTENSE PRESSURE to pass entrance examinations is the knowledge that Japan is a small, crowded country, and that opportunities for successful careers are limited. Once a student has been accepted by a top-ranking university, however, he has little to worry about. He will almost certainly be hired by a large company or a government ministry, and move steadily upward in status. He will not be dismissed except for extreme misbehavior or the grossest incompetence.

Lifetime employment. The principle of lifetime employment was developed by Japan's great commercial-industrial combines known as the zaibatsu. At first it was applied to executives. Promising young men were recruited for managerial positions, trained at company expense, and promised job security with regular pay increases. The object of the zaibatsu was to create a loyal group of managers who would take great pride and satisfaction in their work. Later the principle was extended by the zaibatsu to most of their employees, including blue-collar laborers.

Although the zaibatsu were broken up after World War II, lifetime employment is characteristic of large Japanese companies today. It assures university graduates of secure, middle-class status on the managerial level.

Normally the graduate of a top-ranking university has little difficulty passing a company examination. In any event, his score may be less important to his prospective employers than the school that he attended. If they are alumni of the same school they will usually show a marked preference for him. They assume that he will feel a mutual loyalty and share similar attitudes, making it easier for them to work together harmoniously.

Cooperation and seniority. The Japanese system of employment fosters a spirit of cooperation, rather than competition. Junior executives are recruited after graduation and start work on the same day. They become a distinct company group based on the year they were hired. They go through the same training program and receive the same pay and rank. Throughout their careers, they will advance together in pay and rank, although the more able will be given more important assignments. They will not be asked to serve under anyone from their own group or a younger group. To prevent this from happening, the less able will be retired when they reach the ages of 55 to 60. (Financial loss as a result of early retirement is usually relieved by part-time employment in a subsidiary company.) Only a few members of the group will continue on to the very top, sometimes remaining to a very advanced age.

This system eliminates competition to the group by younger subordinates. A younger man doesn't try to outshine his boss in order to win his job — this would be useless. He may at times disagree with his boss, but in the end he tends to loyally support him. Everyone feels that he is part of a team, and a spirit of cooperation prevails from one level of management to another.

Japanese executives such as this Tokyo businessman enjoy lifetime job security. In return they are expected to be hard-working and loyal to their companies.

The "salary man." An executive with a large company or a government ministry is known in Japan as a "salary man." The term implies that he is a successful white-collar employee who can count on a regular paycheck regardless of economic conditions. Even during a business recession he will not be laid off. In addition, his company or government bureau provides a typical salary man with other benefits that enable him to live well:

• He receives sickness and accident benefits, and a retirement pension. These are important advantages in a country whose public welfare services are inadequate and provide very little assistance.

• Inexpensive company housing may be available to him, as well as a company inn where he may spend his vacations.

• He attends parties and athletic meets sponsored by

189

his company. At least once a year he is treated to an overnight trip to the country with other employees.

• His superiors take a personal interest in his problems both at work and at home. He can call on them to find a school for his daughter, a job for his son, or even to counsel him about problems he may be having with his wife.

A typical salary man enjoys regular working hours and has ample time for leisure. He usually works eight to nine hours a day from Monday to Friday and a half day on Saturday. Most of his leisure activities are with his company work group. After work, for example, he and his group usually stop off at a bar or a coffeehouse to relax for an hour or more. There the tensions that they experience on their jobs tend to be forgotten. Conflicts that have developed in their work are usually smoothed over. They take company trips together by bus or train, and also use these occasions to cement the solidarity of the group. There is often a lot of joking and singing, but there are also opportunities for them to air whatever problems are troubling them.

In return for the company's commitment to him for life, a salary man usually works diligently. He does not object to working overtime without extra compensation if the need arises. As a rule he doesn't take all the vacation time that he is allowed. He would consider that as selfish and disloyal to his work associates and superiors. He is proud to be a member of a large, stable organization and even derives a sense of power from it. He is likely to regard his status as more desirable than that of either the independent businessman or professional.

Is there also a "salary woman" in Japan? Although there are many women executives in small businesses, they are virtually unknown among large companies. In government ministries only a very few women have achieved executive status.

The need to save. By American standards the income of a typical salary man is modest and requires him to live on a tight budget. He must save a large part of his income for his children's education. About three out of four college students attend private institutions. Tuition at a private university may amount to one third of a salary man's annual income. If he has more than one child he has to make great sacrifices for their education. He must also save money if he wants to be comfortable in his old age, for his company pension alone will permit just a bare subsistence standard of living.

Fortunately for the salary man, his wages are paid in a way that makes it fairly easy to save. Twice a year he receives bonuses that are usually 20 to 40 percent of his total income. A typical salary man lives on his regular paycheck and puts his bonuses into a savings account. For most male Japanese the status of a salary man is enviable, and one that they can reasonably aspire to.

The modern samurai. The lifetime commitment of the large company to its employees, and their dedication to the company, remind many Japanese of the country's feudal age. They see the salary man as a modern samurai, ever ready to uphold his company's interests just as the samurai was prepared to back his feudal lord. The most obvious difference, of course, is that the salary man carries a briefcase, not a sword.

The following article describes a typical young salary man's experiences. It is adapted from Edward Norbeck's book *Changing Japan:*

"Jiro received his [law] degree as a student of good but not distinguished standing, well-liked by his professors. The degree rather than individual performance was, he knew, the important thing. He knew also that he was in a favored position for employment. The largest and best corporations, those that paid the highest salaries, provided the most ample fringe benefits, and offered the

191

greatest possibilities for advancement, were within his reach. Campus gossip had told him long ago that the biggest and best firms limited their hiring to graduates of two Tokyo schools, Tokyo University and Hitosubashi* University, and his own Kyoto University. . . .

"His salary would be small at first but would rise as a matter of course as he grew older and acquired a family. Once employed, the prospect of his ever being offered or accepting employment by another firm was small, as was the prospect of being discharged for indifferent or inadequate performance. With luck he might rise to a position as a lesser official. His talents would probably be inadequate to take him further, lacking as he was in social background and influential connections.

"During his final year at the university, Jiro was interviewed for employment by several large business concerns. In January, Asahi* Industries offered him employment after a series of personal interviews and examination of his written personal history, which included extravagant endorsements by his professors. Asahi's scrutiny of his family background showed nothing worse than unexceptional rural poverty. His beginning salary would be more than twice that of his Aunt Shizu* [with whom he lived], and he would receive the equivalent of nearly a half-year's pay annually in bonuses paid in summer and at the end of the year. In addition, he could eat inexpensively at the company dining room and participate in many forms of recreation subsidized by his firm. He could say with pride that he was a salary man employed by Asahi.

"Shacho-san ["the boss" where Jiro worked] offered no objection to his continuing to live with Aunt Shizu. Instead Shacho-san seemed pleased, and sometimes on Saturday afternoons invited Jiro to join him in drinking a glass of beer in his office. But Jiro soon found his lodgings confining. As a young man turning 23, he had tasted few of the pleasures of life and was eager to try them. Shizu herself suggested that it would be better for him to live in the Asahi dormitory, and he quickly agreed. His new quarters, shared by a roommate of the same age, seemed luxurious to him. The large concrete dormitory had a dining room where he could eat and a bath with plenty of hot water. Even the company food seemed delicious. To his great surprise he heard from more sophisticated fellow employees that the food was bad.

"Work went well and was far from difficult. The department head, Mr. Kodama,* was autocratic, and strict seniority prevailed. A lifetime of following rules without hesitation prepared Jiro well to accept the order of things, and he was soon regarded as a trustworthy member of the group. Work proceeded at a leisurely pace, with ample allowances of time for tea and rest. When an important task was entrusted to him, he won the approval of the department head by remaining to work after the customary quitting hour.

"The leisure hours brought much pleasure. Saturday afternoon and Sunday were completely free, and there were many other holidays during the year. . . . He participated in sports with his fellow employees and began setting money aside for a ski outfit. His eagerness led him to heights of thrift as the goal drew near, and he took to going without lunch. Within 18 months he was completely equipped and on a ski train with companions from Asahi. The trip from Osaka was long, but by traveling on the cheapest trains, where they often had to stand, and staying in the cheapest lodges wedged in with companions, the cost was lowered.

"Back in Osaka there were many pleasures, including movies and *sumo** wrestling exhibitions. He met girls employed by Asahi, and through them and his male friends was introduced to still other girls. He discovered the pleasures of coffeehouses and spent long hours in

193

them in groups with other young men and girls, or dating alone. The coffeehouses were especially good when funds were low or when he had a special date. The good coffee shops had "mood," a romantic atmosphere created by elaborate furnishings, soft lights, and music. He could sit for hours over a single tiny cup of coffee, talking or just listening to the music. . . .

"For Jiro these were enjoyable but wholly casual activities. He had no serious romantic interests, and he would not be ready for marriage for several years, when his salary would be adequate. A large part of Jiro's income went to keep himself appropriately dressed. A suit of clothes cost a month's salary or more, although with care it had a long life. As a proper salary man Jiro also needed suitable accessories — expensive cuff links, neckties, and a wristwatch — and he must have sparklingly clean shirts, changed daily without fail. Expenses were high, but Jiro, with an eye to the future, always put aside a sum of money each month. . . ."

Labor unions. The system of lifetime employment in Japan has strongly influenced the organization of labor unions. Instead of separate craft unions, there is one comprehensive union for each large company. It includes blue-collar workers, clerical workers, and junior executives.

Because the company guarantees workers job security, union members tend to identify with the company's interests. They do not want to hurt it economically. They may bargain hard for higher wages and better working conditions, but as a rule they do not engage in prolonged strikes. The number of work days lost in strikes in Japan is less than a third of that in the United States. Union members also do not oppose technological advances because they know that the company will train them in

Top right: Women factory workers such as these
are not part of the lifetime employment system.
Bottom: These workers make high-quality cameras.

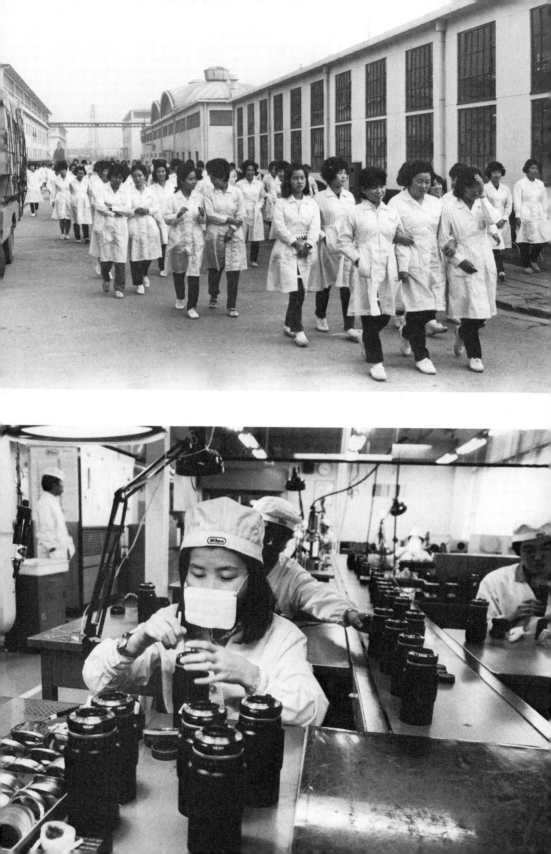

new skills if their old skills are no longer needed.

The company, on its part, wants goodwill and harmony with its permanent force of workers. It is almost as rare for a large company to lay off a permanent worker as it is for Japanese parents to expel a child from the home. As a result, the rate of unemployment in Japan in recent decades has usually been below two percent.

For the large companies, keeping employees on the payroll even during a recession is not a great hardship. If workers were laid off, they would have to be sustained by unemployment benefits financed by taxes on the companies. In the long run the savings to the companies would be minimal.

For the workers the system of job security is much more self-respecting than receiving unemployment compensation. They express their loyalty to the companies that employ them by taking great pride in the quality of their work. There is very little need in Japan for inspectors to check on the performance of factory workers, unlike the situation in many Western nations.

Japanese unions are organized into nationwide federations whose total membership numbers about 12 million workers. This is slightly more than one third of the entire work force, a percentage that is considerably higher than in the United States. Japanese workers are not as committed to their union, however, as American union members. This is largely due to the more personal relationships between bosses and workers in Japanese companies.

The nationwide federations of unions tend to be very active politically. Four-and-a-half million white-collar workers and government employees belong to Sohyo,* a federation that is closely associated with the militant Socialist party. Almost 2½ million blue-collar workers be-

These men are assembling television sets at an electronics factory near Tokyo. The TV's may be sold all over the world.

long to Domei,* a federation that is associated with the more moderate Democratic Socialist party.

The system of lifetime employment sounds almost ideal, but it does not apply to all Japanese workers. Those who are not covered by it are:

• most workers in small plants and in retail stores;
• most women, who have always been considered temporary workers;
• workers with marginal skills in large companies.

The business managers. Japan's top businessmen today are the salaried executives who manage, but do not own, the large corporations. Although their salaries are relatively modest, their positions give them great power and prestige. They also enjoy such privileges as company residences, cars, chauffeurs, luxurious offices, and liberal expense accounts. In traditional Japan a preoccupation with making profits from business activities was regarded as unethical and unpatriotic. To some extent this attitude still persists today. Japan's business managers derive satisfaction not so much from high profits as from the size of their companies, their rate of growth, and the contributions their companies make to the life of the nation.

In pursuing their goal of growth they work very closely with the Japanese government. The powerful Ministry of International Trade and Industry sets production goals for specific industries. It also supervises the acquisition of foreign technology and encourages competition between rival companies. The virtual partnership between the Japanese government and the business community has been a major reason for the country's extraordinary economic success in recent decades. The system is neither capitalistic nor socialistic, but a middle road between the two. Business accepts direction from the government, yet there is ample opportunity for free, competitive enterprise.

Double-check

Review

1. What spirit among workers is fostered by the Japanese system of employment?

2. What is a "salary man"? What does this title imply?

3. What part of the Japanese work force is made up of union members? How does this compare with the United States?

4. List three groups of workers not covered by the Japanese system of lifetime employment.

5. What has been a major reason for Japan's extraordinary economic success in recent decades?

Discussion

1. A Japanese executive once told *Newsweek* magazine: "The company is like the father. It looks after you for your whole life. And you give it devotion." Compare how Japanese workers feel about their company with how you think American workers feel about their company. What are the advantages and disadvantages of each type of relationship?

2. The young man, Jiro, seems to have a fairly good life. Would you like your life to be pretty much like his when you are finished with school? Or do you think he pays too high a price for his apparent security? Explain your answers.

3. Union-management relationships are more cooperative in Japan than in most other highly industrialized countries. What do you think are the reasons for this? Could such a system ever develop in the United States?

Activities

1. Japanese banks and other businesses have branches in the United States. A Japanese from such a business might be invited to speak to the class about the Japanese business system and lifetime employment.

2. Some students might draw cartoons illustrating differences between Japanese and American workers' relationships with their employers.

3. As this chapter points out, "The virtual partnership between the Japanese government and the business community has been a major reason for the country's extraordinary economic success in recent decades." Some students might want to research and report on the high level of cooperation between business and the U.S. government during World War II, when similar "economic miracles" were performed in this country.

Skills

Labor Disputes in Japan and the U.S.*

	U.S.A.	JAPAN
1974	47,991	9,663
1975	31,237	7,974
1976	37,859	3,224
1977	35,822	1,498
1978	36,922	1,353
1979	34,754	919
1980	23,288	998
1981	16,908	543
1982	9,061	535
1983	17,461	504
1984	8,348	354

Source: Bank of Japan. Comparative International Statistics, 1985
*measured in work days lost by individual workers, in thousands.

This chart compares labor disputes of each country. Labor disputes involve protest action, including strikes, walk-outs, and factory shut-downs. Use the chart and information in Chapter 10 to answer the following questions.

1. What years are covered by this chart? What is its source of information?

2. How many days, in thousands, did U.S. workers lose to labor disputes in 1978?

3. In what years did U.S. workers lose fewer days to labor disputes than Japanese workers did in 1974?

4. In what year did Japanese workers lose the fewest days to labor disputes?

5. Recalling what you have learned about Japanese business, how would you explain the comparatively small number of worker days lost to labor disputes in Japan?

Chapter 11

Politics

PERHAPS THE MOST ENDURING American contribution to Japanese society will prove to be a document that was written soon after the end of World War II. This document was, of course, the new constitution drafted for Japan by U.S. occupation authorities. It went into effect in 1947 and was enthusiastically embraced by a great majority of the Japanese people. They welcomed the opportunity to return to democratic rule after years of domination by Japan's authoritarian military leaders. The constitution of 1947 has served them now for more than three decades and is still strongly supported by all but a few political extremists. Most Japanese, in fact, oppose even the slightest revisions to the constitution, for fear that these might open the door to greater changes.

Parliamentary democracy. The 1947 constitution, as we have seen, centered political power in the House of Representatives, the lower house in the Diet. It elects the prime minister, who must be a member of the Diet. He, in turn, selects the members of his cabinet. The prime minister is responsible to the House of Representatives. He can be removed from office at any time that a majority in the lower house votes "no confidence" in his leadership. Instead of resigning, however, the prime minister may declare an end to the session of the lower house and call for new elections in the hope of gaining majority support. This form of representative democracy is patterned after the British system. The Japanese had some experience with it before the military takeover in the 1930's.

The Liberal Democratic Party. In 1955 two conservative political parties that had their origin in the Meiji era combined to form the Liberal Democratic Party (LDP). Until 1978 the LDP held a majority of the seats in the Diet. And although it failed to win an absolute majority in the elections that year, it continued to control the Diet by forming alliances with smaller parties. As a result of this continued control, the LDP has elected all of Japan's prime ministers. But the popular vote received by the LDP has been declining gradually.

For many years, the LDP was able to maintain a very thin majority in the Diet chiefly because the electoral system, which was created in 1947, does not reflect major population shifts that have taken place since then. Rural areas, which strongly support the LDP, still have the same representation in the Diet as they did in 1947, despite a great loss of population. Big city areas, where opposition to the LDP is greatest, have received some additional seats, but not nearly proportionate to the vast increase in urban population. (In 1976 the Supreme Court of Japan ruled that the country's electoral system did not provide political equality and was unconstitutional. As of January 1980, however, the system remained unchanged.)

The LDP is closely allied with big business in Japan and depends heavily on it for financial contributions. As a rule, however, business leaders do not attempt to dictate party politics. The great bulk of LDP voters are in the rural villages, towns, and smaller cities.

The opposition parties. Opposition to the LDP comes mainly from Japan's three leftist parties, the Socialists, the Democratic Socialists, and the Communists. A rising new opposition party is the Komeito,* the political arm of the Soka Gakkai religious movement (see Chapter 7). In 1976 these parties received a combined total of 48.3 percent of the popular vote. The largest share, 20.7 percent, went to the Socialists. Supporters of the opposition parties are heavily concentrated in Japan's great cities, especially Tokyo.

The political views of the three leftist parties derive from the ideas of Karl Marx, the 19th-century philosopher and historian. Generally, however, these parties play down Marx's theory of class conflict. The Japanese, as we have seen, are a very homogeneous people. They do not think of themselves as divided into classes with conflicting interests. If they must specify what class they belong to, more than four out of five will say they are middle class. So Marxist appeals to the interests of the "proletariat" (the working class) make very little impression on the Japanese.

The leftist parties believe in a Socialist economy, but they do not make concrete proposals for government ownership of industries. The Japanese economy has been so successful in recent decades that few people would welcome a change. As a result, the leftist parties concentrate their opposition to the LDP on a variety of side issues, including relations with the United States (see Chapter 6).

Many Japanese who are not Marxists vote for these parties simply to express opposition to the policies of the LDP. Financial support for the leftist parties comes chiefly from the trade unions associated with them.

*One of the Komeito party leaders speaks at
the party's first official meeting in 1964.*

The Japanese influence. Japan's system of parliamentary government was borrowed, of course, from the West. As with so many other cultural borrowings, however, the Japanese have molded it to suit their own characteristics. In the Diet, for example, party members are divided into factions made up of leaders and their personal followers. The relationship between a faction leader and his followers closely resembles that of a benevolent Japanese father toward his dutiful children. The leader, who is a party "strong man," provides his followers with a variety of services and benefits. He may, for example, be the chief source of funds for their election campaigns. In return, they tend to support whatever stands he takes on legislation, and back his efforts to achieve high political office.

The great value that the Japanese place on harmony and consensus is reflected in the way that bills are passed in the Diet. As we have seen, the Japanese do not like majority decisions which, they feel, leave too many people dissatisfied. They prefer that decisions be as nearly unanimous as possible.

If the LDP used its majority in the Diet to ram through controversial legislation, it would run the risk of arousing angry protest demonstrations, such as those that shook the country in 1960 (see Chapter 6). As a result, the LDP seeks to make important bills that it proposes to the Diet as acceptable as possible to the opposition. Its leaders maintain close contacts with the opposition leaders and negotiate with them over proposed legislation long before it is presented to the Diet. Usually the legislation is then modified to meet the objections of the opposition parties. The result of this close cooperation is that almost two thirds of the bills adopted by the Diet are passed unanimously. There is very little debate in the Diet, chiefly because all the issues have been discussed in advance, and also because the Japanese have very little respect for oratory.

Of course, not all legislation passes smoothly. When the opposition decides that a proposed bill is completely unacceptable, it may try to slow down or block the proceedings of the Diet. In extreme cases the speaker of the House of Representatives may be bottled up in his office by force. In turn, as we have seen, the LDP may suddenly call for a vote on a controversial bill when many members of the opposition are absent. In recent years, however, such tactics have become uncommon.

Elections to the lower house. Because power is centered in the House of Representatives, elections to this body are the most important in Japan. Both the system of election and the manner of campaigning differ considerably from our own. Japan is divided into 130 election districts, each with three to five seats in the lower house. In a district with five seats, perhaps eight or more candidates will compete for them. Each voter may choose one candidate on the ballot. The five candidates with the highest number of votes are the winners.

This system increases the chances of minority party candidates being elected. In a five-seat district, for example, a candidate who wins only 20 percent of the total vote is assured of election. While helping small parties, the system creates difficulties for the larger parties. Suppose that the LDP ran four candidates in a district where it had only enough votes to elect three. The LDP votes would then be spread out so thinly among the four candidates that only one or two might be elected, instead of three. So it is essential for a large party to gauge accurately the number of votes it can expect in a district, and not run more candidates than it can elect.

When two or more candidates from the same party bid for seats in an election district, they may compete against each other even more than they do against the candidates of other parties. LDP candidates, for example, often assume that they have little chance of cutting into the Socialist vote. Therefore they compete primarily against each other for the votes of conservatives. As a rule these candidates are attached to rival faction leaders in the Diet.

Because candidates from the same party compete against each other, they must develop personal political organizations to win the support of voters. Quite often a candidate's success is due more to his personal organization than the party label he wears.

Restrictions on campaigning. Japanese election laws place many restrictions on political campaigning. Most of them seem designed to prevent wealthy candidates from gaining an unfair advantage over less affluent candidates, as well as preventing corruption.

However, enforcement of these restrictions is often lax. One provision of the election laws, for example, limits campaign spending to very modest amounts. In 1976 these amounts varied from $16,000 to $55,000, depending upon the number of voters in a district. Some critics claim that these amounts are unrealistically low. In any event, it is an open secret that practically all candidates exceed the legal limits considerably.

The election laws also include these provisions:

• Political campaigning is limited to a period of from three to five weeks before election day.

• Candidates are not allowed to buy time on television or radio, or to buy space for advertisements in newspapers. They are allowed to make three five-minute radio speeches and place five newspaper advertisements that are paid for by the government.

• Door-to-door canvassing for votes is prohibited. So are such activities as running a procession of cars, marching a large group of people, using a siren, employing a band, or making a clamor for the purpose of attracting the attention of voters. The serving of food and drinks for campaign purposes is also forbidden.

• Each candidate may distribute 25,000 campaign postcards to voters, but practically all other written materials, including posters, signs, handbills, and buttons, are forbidden.

• Campaign speeches are subject to numerous regulations. One of them requires candidates to make a number of appearances together to address audiences.

The restrictions on campaigning inevitably produce considerable evasion. One of the most common techniques is for a candidate to call his personal political organization a "cultural club." Its meetings are billed as "study sessions," and his speeches are "educational." In such fashion a candidate may develop support among the voters long before the legal period set for campaigning.

An election campaign. What is a typical Japanese political campaign like? The following description is adapted from the book *Election Campaigning Japanese Style* by Gerald Curtis.

In 1966 the Liberal Democratic Party was shaken by charges of corruption in the government. Among the charges were these:

• A cabinet minister had improperly placed an express railway stop in his district.

• The director of the Defense Agency had used a military band for his own political purposes.

The opposition parties in the House of Representatives demanded new elections to give the voters an opportunity to reject the ruling conservative party. In the cities these demands were backed by large protest demonstrations. Finally, on December 27, the LDP prime minister dissolved the lower house and ordered new elections to be held on January 29, 1967.

One of those who saw an opportunity to win a seat in the lower house was Sato Bunsei,* a 48-year-old conservative from a semirural district in Kyushu. He had narrowly missed being elected to the Diet in 1963 but was confident he would succeed the next time he ran.

Mobilizing support. With the help of two wealthy and influential LDP leaders, Sato maintained a personal political organization in his district. The organization, known as the Wind and Snow Society, described itself as a cultural club. Its activities did, in fact, include reading, mountain climbing, traveling, and "the study of politics and economics." Its main purpose, however, was to mobilize political support for Sato without violating the laws against preelection campaigning. Sato's speeches to the members were billed as "political discussions" or "study sessions."

"I would like to be a symbol of all young women," said actress Akiko Santo in 1974 when she ran for a seat in the Diet.

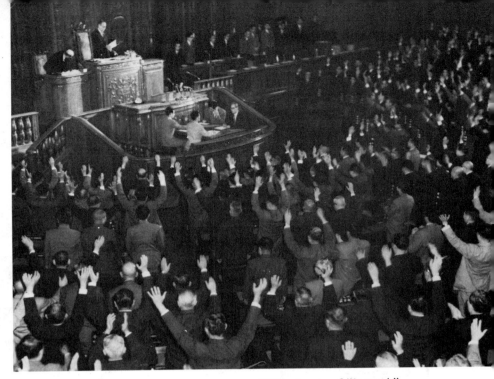

With shouts of "banzai,"
the House of Representatives
dissolves for a new election in 1976.

A major theme of Sato's preelection speeches was the need to "clean up the LDP" and to rid it of the older leaders who were tainted by corruption. Other speakers would praise Sato as one of the young, progressive conservatives who should be given a chance to modernize the party. No one, of course, could mention that Sato would actually be a candidate in the next election. On one occasion Sato's wife appealed to a group of women voters in these words:

"Sato is a truly rare person. As an egg of a politician, this is a golden egg. I have one favor to ask of you — help hatch this golden egg."

At the headquarters of the Wind and Snow Society, Sato received a stream of visitors from early morning to late at night. Most were seeking some kind of favor or service. Could he find jobs for them? Could he help their children get into a high school? Could he find eligible suitors for their daughters? Sato promised to do his best for them all and was often successful.

Sato did other favors for the voters in his district. He attended numerous weddings, sent wreaths to funerals, and sent packages of incense to families that observed the annual festival in honor of the dead. In addition, he contributed a large amount of money to build a new roof on a Buddhist temple, and to erect a statue of a local hero.

The goal that Sato was working toward — a seat in the House of Representatives — came closer when the lower house was dissolved and new elections were scheduled for January 29.

Sato is warned. In order to run, however, Sato first had to win the endorsement of his party. His candidacy was bitterly opposed by the two incumbent LDP representatives from his district, Ayabe* and Nishimura.* They argued that Sato had been disloyal to the party and should not be allowed to run. Sato finally won the party's endorsement but was warned "to abstain from making antiparty speeches and to campaign in harmony with your elders from the district, Ayabe and Nishimura."

Sato, however, ignored the warning. When the official campaign began on January 8, he continued to stress the need to "purify" and "rejuvenate" the LDP. He also expressed his concern for the "little man" and called for increased welfare legislation to protect "the young, the elderly, and the mute."

Sato's district had three seats in the House of Representatives. Five candidates were competing for them. In addition to the three LDP candidates, there was one Socialist, Komatsu,* who was seeking reelection, and one Communist, Tsuru.* At the beginning of the campaign the newspapers predicted that the two LDP incumbents, Ayabe and Nishimura, would win easily. The third seat was a toss-up between Sato and Komatsu.

Public opinion polls soon revealed, however, that Sato's strategy of campaigning against corruption in the

LDP was attracting many conservative voters. Both his LDP opponents were forced to go on the defensive. Ayabe told his audiences that a few isolated incidents of corruption should not be allowed to blacken the name of the LDP and the great majority of its members.

"There has been a lot of talk of a black mist [scandal], but I have been honest and clean," Ayabe said. "Please, reelect an honest politician."

An American technique. During the last three days of the campaign Sato decided to use a technique that was more characteristic of American politicians than Japanese. He had heard that President John F. Kennedy shook the hands of so many voters during his campaign that he needed injections to lessen the pain. Sato planned to shake the hands of at least 9,000 people in Beppu,* the largest town in his district. On the evening before the election Sato proudly displayed a raw and swollen right hand.

Sato's tactics proved remarkably effective. He not only won election to the lower house, but he received more votes than any other candidate. The other two winners from his district were Komatsu and Nishimura. The final results were as follows:

Candidate and party	Votes
1. Sato (LDP)	60,293
2. Komatsu (Socialist)	59,919
3. Nishimura (LDP)	51,815
4. Ayabe (LDP)	49,547
5. Tsuru (Communist)	5,055

More than 80 percent of the eligible voters in Sato's district took part in the election. This was higher than the national average of 70–75 percent and far more than the American average of 50–60 percent.

212

Double-check

Review

1. In which house of the Diet is political power centered?

2. Which Japanese political party has held a majority of the seats in the Diet since 1955?

3. Why is there very little debate in the Diet?

4. What was the main purpose of the Wind and Snow Society?

5. What percent of eligible voters in Japan vote in elections? How does this compare with the U.S. average?

Discussion

1. What similarities are there between political parties in the U.S. and in Japan? What are some of the major differences?

2. Although Japan's leftist parties have lately grown in strength, none of them ever seems to get enough votes to form a government. Does the electoral system itself have something to do with this? Are there factors in Japanese history and culture that work against these parties? Explain.

3. Japan's election laws place severe restrictions on political campaigns. Do you think these laws are good for Japan? Why? Would such laws be good for the United States? Why, or why not?

Activities

1. Who is the current Japanese prime minister? To which political party does he belong? When and how did he come to power? What are his views on relations with the United States? A committee of students might watch TV, newspapers, and magazines for reports on these and other current political developments in Japan. Members of the committee could make brief oral reports on some matters and post clippings on a bulletin board.

2. Two or more students might role-play a conversation between a candidate for a seat in the Japanese House of Representatives and his campaign manager in which they discuss ways to get around the strict campaign restrictions without actually breaking the law.

3. Three or more students might play the roles of leftist, liberal, and conservative candidates for election to the Diet. Each should give a short speech to the class on how he or she would vote on two of the following: a bill to increase the defense budget; a bill to increase controls on industrial pollution; a bill to increase urban representation in the Diet. The rest of the class could ask questions and then vote for a candidate.

Skills

MEMBERS OF HOUSE OF REPRESENTATIVES AND HOUSE OF COUNCILLORS BY PARTY
(March 31, 1978)

House of Representatives		House of Councillors	
Party	Members	Party	Members
Total	511	Total	252
Liberal Democrat	254	Liberal Democrat	124
Socialist	119	Socialist	53
Komeito	56	Komeito	28
Democratic Socialist	28	Communist	16
Communist	19	Democratic Socialist	11
New Liberal Club	17	New Liberal Club	5
Independent	4	Dai-ni-in Club	5
Other	6	Other	7
Vacancies	8	Vacancies	3

Source: Japanese Ministry of Home Affairs

Use the table above and information in Chapter 11 to answer the following questions.

1. Which party has members in the House of Councillors but not in the House of Representatives?

(a) New Liberal Club   (b) Communist   (c) *Dai-ni-in* Club

2. Which party has the largest number of members in the House of Representatives?

(a) Socialist   (b) Communist   (c) Liberal Democrat

3. What proportion of the members of the House of Councillors are Liberal Democrats?

(a) one half   (b) more than half   (c) less than half

4. How many additional votes would the Liberal Democrats need to control a majority in the House of Representatives?

(a) four   (b) one   (c) two

5. Recalling what you have learned about Japanese politics, give two reasons why control of a majority in the House of Representatives is important to a party.

Chapter 12

Mass Culture

ON WARM SUNDAY AFTERNOONS in Tokyo, hundreds of teenagers assemble in the streets and parks for informal dancing. They wear their most outrageous Western-style clothes, which often imitate American fashions of the 1950's. Rock and jazz music from all eras plays on huge radio-cassette decks.

Mass enthusiasm for popular music is characteristic of modern, industrial society, especially among young people. So are such popular leisure activities as reading newspapers and magazines, watching television, skiing, sightseeing, taking pictures, and many others. Leisure activities that are pursued by millions of people in modern societies are often referred to as "mass culture".

The Japanese are as inclined to mass enthusiasm as Americans are, and in some ways outdo Americans. Mass culture in Japan has been stimulated greatly by the nation's postwar "economic miracle." It produced both the high standard of living and much of the technology that makes leisure possible for large numbers of people. Let's examine some of the major forms of mass culture in Japan and see how they influence and reflect that society.

215

Television. In 1960 less than one Japanese household out of four had a television set. Today practically every household has at least one set, and most have color TV's. The Japanese watch television, which they call *terebi,** an average of three hours a day.

Japan has two government networks, known as **NHK**, supported by a tax on TV sets. One broadcasts educational programs, including instruction in foreign languages and mathematics. The other competes with five private networks in presenting general-interest programs such as news, drama, comedy, and quiz shows.

Japanese television fare is varied and includes some American movies and TV shows with dubbed-in Japanese voices. While American television is less popular than in the 1970's, Japanese viewers can still watch shows as varied as *Little House on the Prairie, Cagney and Lacey,* and a video show modeled after MTV.

Television has done a great deal to blur the differences in values and attitudes that once divided rural and urban Japan. By presenting almost identical programming, it has contributed to uniformity in Japanese life. Professor Fukutake of the University of Tokyo made the following comment about the pervasive effects of TV:

"Television can disseminate a vast amount of information, and the effect on those who receive it may be to create a people with standardized tastes, behavior, and thinking. If most people watch and listen to low-level programs with little intellectual or moral value, we may be encouraging a mass degeneration of intellectual interest and capacity. If, on the other hand, television can inspire new aspirations and standards of thinking, it will assist in the transition to a modern and humane society. The potential to learn is strong in every viewer. But if commercial programs exploit the human interest in vul-

Imported from the U.S., baseball is now played and watched by millions of Japanese.

gar amusement and sensationalism, they are performing a great disservice to the people. Then this medium cannot become an uplifting force in mass culture."

The NHK educational network has been experimenting with a unique system known as two-way community television. This system enables home viewers to communicate directly with the studio and to participate in programs. By pressing buttons on an electronic device, viewers can link their sets to a studio computer that provides a wide range of information. Viewers can ask for medical advice, sports results, community news, weather forecasts, recipes, shopping tips, etc. The information is then flashed on viewers' TV screens.

Viewers are also taught at home by studio teachers with whom they can converse. They can be tested quickly to see how well they are learning. A teacher, for example, gives viewers a multiple-choice question. They answer by pressing a button. The answers are then fed into a minicomputer, letting the teacher know almost immediately how much the viewers have understood.

Viewers can also select a wide variety of entertainment. By pressing a combination of buttons they may see popular stories, travel films, or even have their fortunes told. In addition, there is an original one-hour show each day in which members of the community provide entertainment.

Newspapers. The Japanese are exceptionally avid readers, a fact that is reflected in the huge circulations of their newspapers. Average daily newspaper circulation amounts to slightly more than 500 for every 1,000 persons, a ratio that is among the highest in the world and almost twice that of the United States. Because Japan is a small country, its major newspapers are either national or regional, rather than local. The three largest national

A fairly common bookstore scene —
avid readers try to make a choice.

newspapers, which are all based in Tokyo, are *Asahi,* *Yomiuri,** and *Mainichi.** They publish both morning and evening editions. The morning circulations of these newspapers are as follows:

Asahi — close to 6 million;

Yomiuri — about 4½ million;

Mainichi — 3½ million.

The evening circulations of these newspapers amount to more than half of the morning editions. All three are printed in several locations throughout Japan and distributed almost entirely by home delivery.

Japanese newspapers usually have fewer pages than metropolitan papers in the United States. Morning editions may have 24 pages; evening editions, less. They carry relatively little advertising, however, so there is a high proportion of news and other features.

Perhaps the most striking aspect of Japanese newspapers is their sameness. Virtually the same news appears on almost the same pages of every newspaper. The next to the last page of each, for example, is always devoted to news of crime, accidents, and human-interest stories. The papers have very few interpretive or analytical articles, and even their editorials seem to copy one another. The result is that tens of millions of Japanese tend to view the world with similar attitudes and opinions.

Despite their sameness Japanese newspapers maintain high journalistic standards. They have large numbers of reporters who provide full coverage of both national and international news, and stories are carefully edited to make sure they are accurate. In the rest of the world very few newspapers surpass the Japanese national dailies in either the amount or quality of news presentation.

All major Japanese newspapers claim to be neutral politically. In reality, however, most of them lean slightly to the left and tend to be critical of Japan's conservative government. This is due partly to the fact that the papers are produced in the nation's great metropolitan centers, where opposition to the ruling conservative party is highest. But it also stems from an old tradition in Japanese newspaper publishing that goes back to Meiji times. During that period, when newspapers began to develop and flourish, many of the publishers were former samurai who resented being excluded from the group that controlled the government. They became critics of the powerful Meiji leaders. Since then, except for the 1930's and World War II when Japan's military leaders suppressed all opposition, the press has usually taken a critical attitude toward Japanese governments.

Magazines. Since the 1950's the number of magazines in Japan has increased enormously. They offer much more variety than the newspapers, but their circulations generally are smaller. The top three weeklies claim to have more than a half-million readers each. A few monthlies are general-interest magazines that feature serious articles. A large number of the weeklies are specialty magazines covering a wide range of interests from sports to knitting. Others tend to be sensational and deal in gossip about celebrities. Professor Fukutake made this observation about some Japanese magazines:

"The sports tabloids, which also supply much news concerning mass amusements, are widely read for their specialist treatment. While many professional baseball players are well-known, a great many people probably cannot recall the names of today's cabinet ministers. People are avidly interested in TV personalities, and weekly magazines carrying articles on their private lives sell extraordinarily well. A story about the marital difficulties of a famous star attracts more interest than a crucial remark by a cabinet minister."

Unlike the newspapers, most general-interest magazines do not claim to be politically neutral. Many are quite frankly biased in favor of one view or another.

Books. The end of World War II produced an immediate boom in the publication of books in Japan. Released from the severe restrictions of wartime controls and promised freedom of expression, writers rushed to complete manuscripts and get them into print. Some publishers anticipated the boom and got off to a quick start. The head of one company decided on August 14, 1945, the day that Emperor Hirohito announced Japan's surrender, to publish a new Japanese-English dictionary. It was completed within a month and soon sold more than three million copies.

There was a strong demand at first for new translations of Western literature. U.S. authors had not been very popular in Japan before the war, but now the Japanese began to explore seriously the works of Ernest Hemingway, William Faulkner, and others. U.S. bestsellers about World War II, such as John Hersey's *Hiroshima* and Norman Mailer's *The Naked and the Dead*, enjoyed great popularity in Japan.

Japanese literature also showed great vitality as it reached out to a truly mass audience. Novels reflected the demoralization of the Japanese people at the end of the war, and some were harshly critical of the army. In *Zone of Emptiness* by Noma Hiroshi,* for example, an ex-officer denounces the corruption that he has seen in Japan's home forces during the war:

"The army of the interior is rotten to the core, to the very core. When I was overseas, I used to hear it said that the army of the interior had preserved the old traditions of honor and dignity ... unfortunately, when I returned I realized that this was completely untrue, that everything was worse than I could have imagined. At first, I did what I could, as an officer, to maintain standards. That's what caused my downfall. I loved the army with all my heart. It was impossible for me to tolerate the people who jeered at it and besmirched it, but then

I found myself coming up against powerful obstacles, colonels, majors. . . . It's all a matter of pleasing your superiors. . . . The supplies that are delivered go straight to the commanding officer, who uses them for making personal gifts. . . . I was unable to put up with such corruption. I tried to do something about it, but I was beaten. It's too big a job for one man. . . . I was kicked out."

In more recent years a familiar theme of Japanese novelists is the desire to escape from the pressures of modern, industrial society. In the works of Oe Kenzaburo,* for example, individuals are trapped by the demands of a society that seems to have no other purpose than economic growth. Kenzaburo's 1964 novel *A Personal Matter* broadly depicts postwar Japan as the land of "economic animals" who have poured their souls into transistor radios.

Movies. The postwar period developed into a golden age for Japanese moviemakers. The major movie studios had not been seriously damaged in the war. The occupation authorities encouraged the film industry to expand in order to provide entertainment for a people who sorely needed it. At first nearly 40 percent of the movie houses in Japan showed nothing but American films. Day after day they attracted capacity audiences. Within a short time the process was somewhat reversed. The Japanese began to produce movies that ranked with the best in the world, and many of them were seen — and acclaimed — in the United States.

Among the most popular films in Japan and abroad were those of the director Kurosawa Akira.* These films included *Rashomon,* *To Live*, and *Seven Samurai*.

Seven Samurai was released in 1954. It tells the story of a group of ronin (masterless samurai) in Tokugawa times who are hired to defend a village against marauding bandits. In brutal fighting that at times causes them to question their most basic values, the group finally

223

A scene from Rashomon, *winner of the Grand Prize at the 1951 Venice Film Festival.*

drives off the bandits. *Seven Samurai* is much more than an exciting action movie. It reflects the traditional Japanese sensitivity to the forces of nature and the passing seasons, which underscore the uncertainty of human life. At the film's end the villagers must begin spring planting, while the surviving samurai once again become ronin, to follow a rootless, meaningless existence.

In recent years moviemaking in Japan has declined because of the growing competition of television. Many movie theaters have gone out of business, and the major studios have been reduced to turning out low-budget "junk" films. A few independent producers struggle to keep alive the high artistic standards achieved in the golden age after World War II.

Sports. Practically every Western form of athletics is enjoyed in Japan, as well as a number of native sports.

The most popular Western sport is baseball, which the Japanese call *basuboru*.* There are two professional leagues, the Central and the Pacific, with six clubs each. All 12 clubs have English nicknames such as Giants, Dragons, and Whales. Baseball is also played widely in schools and colleges, and among workers.

Other popular Western sports are volleyball, swimming, and skiing. Lately bowling has caught on with the young, while golf has been taken up mainly by the well-to-do. On Japanese golf courses women serve as caddies.

The most popular native sport is *sumo* wrestling, which may be 2,000 years old. It is vaguely associated with Shinto rites and mysteries, and the referee wears robes similar to a priest's. The contestants wear only

Sumo wrestling matches begin quite formally.

loincloths and tie their hair up in the traditional Japanese top-knot. Sumo wrestlers are immensely heavy and strong, and are taller than most Japanese men. At the peak of his career a star sumo wrestler will weigh about 310 pounds and will have a huge belly, big buttocks, and very thick thighs.

The object of a sumo wrestling match is for a contestant to make some part of his opponent's body (other than the feet) touch the ground, or else to force him out of the ring entirely. The matches are often brief, and the preliminary posturing of the opponents may be more entertaining than the actual wrestling. Before the match begins the contestants glare at each other fiercely, squat and rise, and flex their muscles. Each transfers his weight to one leg and raises the other high in the air to one side. These actions are intended, of course, to intimidate opponents. Sumo wrestling makes a lively televison show, and its popularity has increased as a result. Sumo champions have huge followings in the main cities.

Mass culture thrives in many forms in modern Japan. In the summer an endless chain of people climbs Mount Fuji.* On hot weekends millions of people go swimming at the Shonan* beaches near Tokyo. In the spring and fall sightseers swarm to famous places of beauty. In the winters ski slopes are dangerously overcrowded. City amusement areas have thousands of bars, cafés, and restaurants that are usually filled with people. And huge department stores that offer a wide variety of goods attract large numbers of customers.

Japan's cultural identity. Since the end of World War II, Japan has been flooded by Western mass culture, especially from the United States. The latest evidence was the completion in 1985 of a 204-acre Disneyland near Tokyo. The park, which is already quite popular, is a replica of its American counterparts.

Will Japanese culture ultimately become indistinguishable from our own? Most students of Japanese history doubt it. In premodern times, they say, Japan borrowed heavily from Chinese culture. More recently, during the Meiji era, Japan borrowed extensively from the culture of the West. Yet almost always the Japanese molded and adapted whatever they borrowed to suit their own tastes and purposes. By the same process the Japanese are likely to retain their distinctive cultural identity now and in the future.

Japanese people enjoy modern life, but they still honor their cultural traditions with activities such as this festival at the Asakusa Shrine in Tokyo.

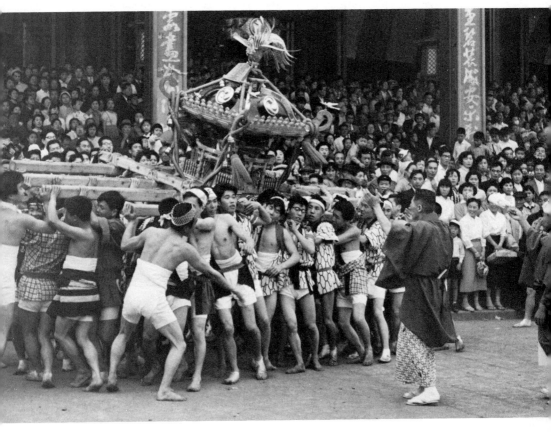

Double-check

Review

1. What effect has television had on the values and attitudes of rural and urban Japan?

2. Where does Japan rank among nations in average daily newspaper circulation per 1,000 persons? How does Japan's ratio compare with that of the United States?

3. What has been a familiar theme of recent Japanese novelists?

4. What traditional Japanese attitudes are reflected in the popular film *Seven Samurai?*

5. What have the Japanese almost always done with whatever they have borrowed from other cultures?

Discussion

1. This chapter points out that television "has done a great deal to blur the differences in values and attitudes that once divided rural and urban Japan." Do you think these developments are good or bad, or neither, for Japanese society? How are these developments similar to or different from television's effect on values and attitudes in the United States?

2. In recent years Japan has been flooded by Western mass culture, especially American — from TV programs to sports to Disneyland. Why do you think this has happened? How might this be good for Japan? How might it be bad? Why do you think the reverse has not happened? Explain.

3. What image of the United States do you think the average Japanese man or woman gets from the mass culture we export to Japan?

Activities

1. Some students might research and report on the history and symbolism of sumo wrestling. Then some students might take turns acting out the preliminary ritual posturing of sumo wrestlers.

2. The entire class might pretend that it has been asked by the U.S. government to select examples of U.S. culture to be sent to Japan next month. You may send five of each of the following: books, records, movies, magazines, and TV shows. Which ones would you send? Discuss and vote.

3. The entire class might plan a one-month trip to Japan. List the cities and other areas you would like to visit. Name the sites, works of art, buildings, etc., that you would like to see. Prepare questions to ask the people you would meet.

Skills

JAPANESE PARTICIPATION RATES BY AGE IN THREE SPORTS IN 1976

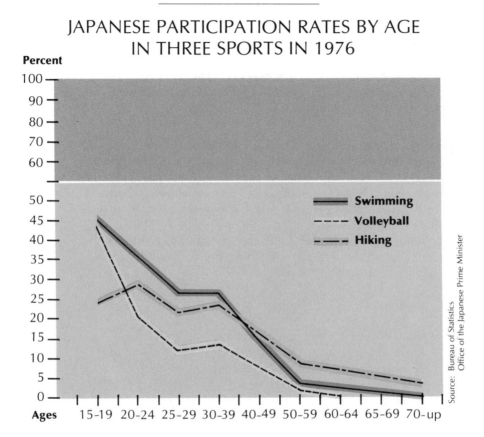

Use the line graph above and information in Chapter 12 to answer the following questions.

1. What does the break in the graph show?

2. How many age categories are shown on this graph? For what age group is information not given?

3. What percentage of Japanese people between the ages of 15 and 19 took part in swimming during 1976?

4. Does participation in these three sports generally increase or decrease as people get older? In which sport does participation decrease the least?

5. Judging from this graph, at which location would you stand a better chance of meeting someone over 70 years old — Mount Fuji or Shonan? On what do you base your answer?

Pronunciation Guide

Japanese words and names that are familiar to Americans and are found in Webster's dictionary are accented as the dictionary indicates. Unfamiliar words and names that do *not* appear in the dictionary are left unaccented, since the subtleties in accenting spoken Japanese need concern only those who undertake a serious study of the language.

The following system translates each syllable into the nearest common English equivalent. Syllables set in capitals are accented. Principal sound equivalents are:

a (as in cat)	oh (as in flow)
ah (as in odd)	on (as in on)
ai (as in eye)	oo (as in too)
ay (as in bay)	or (as in for)
ch (as in chair)	oy (as in boy)
e (as in silent)	s (as in sit)
ee (as in eat)	sh (as in ship)
eh (as in end)	t (as in tin)
ew (as in new)	th (as in then)
g (as in go)	u (as in foot)
ih (as in trip)	uh (as in circus)
j (as in jaw)	y (as in yet)
k (as in keep)	z (as in zebra)

Ainu — AI-new
Amaterasu — ah-mah-tay-rah-soo
Amida Buddha — ah-mee-dah BOO-dah
Asahi — ah-sah-hee
Ashikaga — ah-shee-kah-gah
Atsuko Anzai — aht-soo-koh ahn-zai
Ayabe — ah-yah-bay
Basho — bah-shoh
basuboru — bay-soo-boh-roo
Beppu — BEHP-oo
Bikini — be-KEE-nee

Buddhism — BOO-dihz-uhm
Bunchana Atthakor — bun-CHAH-nah at-TAH-kor
bunraku — buhn-rahk-oo
bushido — BUSH-ih-doh
Chisso — chee-soh
Choshu — choh-shoo
Confucianism — kuhn-FYOO-shahn-ihz-uhm
daimyo — DAI-mee-oh
Domei — DOH-may
Edo — eh-doh
Fuji — FOO-jee
Fujiwara — foo-jee-wah-rah
Fujiyama — foo-jee-YAH-mah
Fukutake — foo-kuh-tah-kay
futon — foo-tohn
geisha — GAY-shah
genro — GEN-roh
gohan — goh-hahn
haiku — HAI-koo
hakama — hah-kah-mah
harakiri — har-ih-KIHR-ee
Heian — hay-on
hibachi — hih-BAHCH-ee
Hideyoshi — hee-day-yoh-shee
Hiei — hee-yay
Hirohito — hihr-oh-HEE-toh
Hiroshima — hihr-oh-SHEE-mah
Hitosubashi — hee-toh-soo-bah-shee
Hokkaido — hoh-KAI-doh
Honshu — HON-shoo
Ikeda — ee-KAY-dah
Inukai — ee-new-kai
Izanagi — ee-zah-nah-gee
Izanami — ee-zah-nah-mee
Jihpen — jer-buhn
Jimmu — jee-moo
jozu — joh-zoo
judo — JOOD-oh
kabuki — kah-BOO-kee
Kamakura — kah-mah-KOO-rah
kami — kah-mee
kamikaze — kahm-ih-KAHZ-ee
kana — kah-nah

kimono — kah-MOH-noh
Kishi — kee-shee
koan — koh-ahn
Kodama — koh-dah-mah
Komatsu — koh-maht-soo
Komeito — koh-may-toh
kotatsu — koh-taht-soo
Kurosawa Akira — koo-roh-sah-wah ay-kee-rah
kun — koon
Kyoto — kee-OH-toh
Kyushu — kee-OO-shoo
Mainichi — mah-ee-nee-chee
Manchukuo — man-CHOO-kwoh
Masao — mah-sah-oh
Meiji — may-ee-jee
Minamoto Yoritomo — mee-nah-moh-toh yoh-ree-toh-moh
Minamata — mee-nah-mah-tah
Mishima Yukio — mee-shih-mah yoo-kee-oh
miso-shiru — mee-soh-shee-roo
Mitsubishi — meet-soo-bee-shee
Mitsui — met-soo-ee
mobo — moh-boh
moga — moh-gah
Murasaki Shikibu — moor-ah-SAH-kee she-kee-boo
Mutsuhito — moot-suh-hee-toh
Nagasaki — nahg-ah-SAHK-ee
Nara — NAHR-ah
Nihon — nee-hahn
Ninigi — nee-NEE-gee
Nishimura — nee-shee-moo-rah
No — noh
Noma Hiroshi — noh-mah hee-roh-shee
Oda Nobunaga — oh-dah noh-boo-nah-gah
Oe Kenzaburo — oh-ay ken-zah-boo-roh
Okinawa — oh-kah-NAH-wah
okusan — oh-koo-sahn
Onoda — oh-noh-dah
o-riko — oh-ree-koh
Osaka — oh-SAHK-ah
otochan — oh-toh-chan
Pimiko — pee-mee-koh
Rashomon — rah-show-mohn
ronin — roh-neen

Sakhalin — SAK-ah-leen
sake — SAHK-ee
samurai — SAM-ah-rai
san — sahn
sansankudo — sahn-sahn-ku-doh
Sato Bunsei — sah-toh boon-say
sensei — sen-say
seppuku — se-POO-koo
Shacho-san — sha-choh-sahn
Shikoku — shi-KOH-koo
Shinto — SHIHN-toh
Shizu — shee-zoo
shogun — SHOH-guhn
shogunate — SHOH-guhn-uht
Shonan — shoh-nahn
Shotoku — shoh-toh-koo
Sohyo — soh-hyoh
Soka Gakkai — soh-kah gahk-ai
sukiyaki — soo-kee-YAHK-ee
sumo — SOO-moh
Suzuki — soo-zoo-kee
Suzuki-san — soo-zoo-kee-sahn
Tadashi Fukutake — Tah-dah-shee foo-koo-tah-kay
Tanaka — tah-nahk-ah
Tanaka-kun — tah-nahk-ah-koon
tanka — TAHN-kah
tatami — tah-tahm-ee
terebi — teh-reh-bee
Todaiji — toh-dai-jee
tokonoma — toh-koh-NOH-mah
Tokugawa Ieyasu — toh-koo-gah-wah ee-yay-yah-soo
Tokyo — TOH-kee-oh
Toshio Hashimoto — toh-shee-oh hah-shee-moh-toh
tsuno-kakushi — tsoo-noh-kah-koo-shee
Tsuru — tsoo-roo
Wa — wah
Yamato — yah-MAH-toh
yen — yen
Yokohama — yoh-kah-HAHM-ah
Yokoi — yoh-koh-ee
Yomiuri — yoh-mee-oo-ree
zaibatsu — zai-baht-soo
Zen — zen

Index